A GUIDE TO

MEASURE FOR MEASURE

The Shakespeare Handbooks

Guides available now:

- Antony & Cleopatra
- As You Like It
- Hamlet
- Henry IV, Part 1
- Julius Caesar
- King Lear
- Macbeth
- Measure for Measure
- The Merchant of Venice
- A Midsummer Night's Dream
- Othello
- Romeo & Juliet
- The Tempest
- Twelfth Night

Further titles in preparation.

The Shakespeare Handbooks

A Guide to
Measure for Measure

by Alistair McCallum

Upstart Crow Publications

First published in 2019 by
Upstart Crow Publications

Copyright © Alistair McCallum 2019

All rights reserved

A CIP catalogue record for this book
is available from the British Library

ISBN 978 1 899747 14 6

Printed in Great Britain by Print2Demand Ltd,
1 Newlands Road, Westoning,
Bedfordshire MK45 5LD

www.shakespeare-handbooks.com

Setting the scene

Shakespeare wrote *Measure for Measure* in the period 1603–4, when he was about forty years old. He was a leading member of the King's Men, London's most successful theatre company. He was also a shareholder in the company and in its new venture, the Globe Theatre, which had been the company's home since the start of the century.

With the newly crowned King James I as their patron, Shakespeare and his colleagues were frequent performers at court, and at state occasions and celebrations. However, theatre remained a precarious business, and in 1603 all the London theatres were closed for the entire season due to an outbreak of plague. It seems likely that *Measure for Measure* was one of the first plays to be performed in the reopened Globe in the summer of 1604.

Unlike Shakespeare's earlier comedies, *Measure for Measure* is a dark, cynical, probing drama, at times coming close to tragedy. Various critics have labelled it a 'problem play', a 'bitter comedy' and a 'tragicomedy', and there has been much speculation about the personal and professional factors that were influencing Shakespeare during this transitional period in his career.

Measure for Measure is a drama that deals with powerful, conflicting ideas and arguments. Watching the play is a demanding, challenging but ultimately rewarding experience:

"*Measure for Measure is the last comedy Shakespeare wrote. After it comes an unbroken succession of tragedies ... Sombre in tone, it creates images of human folly and cruelty which seem at moments to overstep the limits of comic form ... The play anatomizes society. It scrutinizes man's claims to justice, rationality and self-control ... Difficult to interpret,* Measure for Measure *has provoked more critical disagreement, and a greater number of conflicting readings, than any other Shakespeare comedy.*"

    Anne Barton, Royal Shakespeare Company programme notes, 1970

An enigma

Duke Vincentio, ruler of the city-state of Vienna, is anxious.

A naturally withdrawn, contemplative character, he is concerned that he has not been paying enough attention to the condition of his city. He suspects that moral standards may have been allowed to slip, and he intends to investigate.

With this in mind, he has decided to absent himself from Viennese political life for a while. But where is he going? What is he going to do? And who is he going to leave in charge while he is away?

Curtain up

A sudden departure I, i

Duke Vincentio is talking to his trusted adviser Escalus. He is about to bestow an important responsibility on the elderly nobleman, but he has no qualms about his decision. He is confident that Escalus, with his long experience of Viennese politics, needs no advice from him:

Duke: Of government the properties to unfold
Would seem in me t'affect speech and discourse,[1]
Since I am put to know that your own science
Exceeds, in that, the lists of all advice
My strength can give you.[2]
                    ... The nature of our people,
Our city's institutions, and the terms
For common justice, y'are as pregnant in
As art and practice hath enriched any
That we remember.[3]

[1] *it would be presumptuous of me to explain the nature of government to you*
[2] *I have to acknowledge that your understanding of the subject goes beyond the bounds of any advice that I can give you*
[3] *you are as well versed in these matters, both in theory and through experience, as anyone in living memory*

The Duke now mentions his plan. He has to leave Vienna shortly, he explains, and has decided that Lord Angelo is to rule in his absence, with Escalus as his second in command. Angelo is the best man for the job, agrees Escalus; and at this moment Angelo himself appears.

The Duke begins by complimenting Angelo on his undoubted virtues. It is only right, he asserts, that such noble qualities should be used to good effect rather than simply be admired:

> *Duke:* Heaven doth with us as we with torches do,
> Not light them for themselves; for if our virtues
> Did not go forth of us, 'twere all alike
> As if we had them not.[1]
>
> [1] *if we did not make good use of our virtues, there would be no point in possessing them*

An important duty is to be conferred on Angelo, announces the Duke solemnly. He will rule Vienna in the Duke's absence, with the power of life and death over its citizens:

> *Duke:* In our remove, be thou at full ourself.[1]
> Mortality and mercy in Vienna
> Live in thy tongue, and heart.
>
> [1] *while I am away, you will fully take over my role*

Angelo, taken aback, asks whether there is any way in which he can prove his worth before taking on such an important task. The Duke brushes aside Angelo's fears: he has thought about the matter and made his decision, he states, and needs to leave at once.

While the Duke is away, he intends to communicate with Angelo by letter from time to time. He emphasises, however, that Angelo is to rely on his own judgement:

> *Duke:* Your scope is as mine own,
> So to enforce or qualify the laws
> As to your soul seems good.

In 1603, after 45 years on the throne of England, Queen Elizabeth I died. It soon became clear that her successor, King James I, was a great theatre enthusiast; just ten days after taking the throne, he announced his decision to become the official patron of Shakespeare's acting company.

While this gave the company unprecedented prestige and security, it meant a much heavier workload; the actors could be called on at short notice to perform at royal events and state occasions of all kinds, and new work was constantly in demand.

The king's tastes and interests had to be considered, too. He was known, from his published works, to be particularly interested in the nature and philosophy of monarchy, and believed firmly in the king's God-given authority over his people. However, Shakespeare's treatment of such topics is far from uncritical:

"Though the playwright seems to have felt it necessary to respond to the King's keen interests in theology and justice, the plays he produced in the first years of James's reign are not hollow royalist propaganda ... Every play Shakespeare wrote in the first years of James's reign seems touched by the same forces – at once subject to a demanding royal scrutiny, yet never subservient to it. Measure for Measure *responds in a characteristically oblique way to questions James had outlined in his own published treatise on kingship. Almost the play's first words are 'of government', as if we are about to hear an official policy paper read out ... These circumlocutory words are spoken by Duke Vincentio; in the first of many surprises sprung by the play, his unorthodox solution to the fact that his city, Vienna, is so chaotically governed is to propose fleeing it, leaving his deputies in charge with the minimum of guidance."*

Andrew Dickson, *Royal Shakespeare: A Playwright and his King*, 2016

The Duke now bids a hasty farewell. As he leaves, he mentions that he will depart from Vienna discreetly. He dislikes ostentatious public ceremonies, and distrusts those who enjoy such things:

> *Duke:* ... I'll privily away.[1] I love the people,
> But do not like to stage me to their eyes:
> Though it do well, I do not relish well
> Their loud applause and *aves*[2] vehement;
> Nor do I think the man of safe discretion
> That does affect it.[3]
>
> [1] *I will leave unobtrusively*
> [2] *cheers, cries of acclamation*
> [3] *in my opinion, any man who is fond of public adulation is not trustworthy*

With that, the Duke hurries away. Angelo and Escalus turn to one another. They agree that the next step is clear: they urgently need to discuss the roles that have suddenly been thrust upon them.

A new regime I, ii

In a street in Vienna, the libertine Lucio is chatting to two of his friends. The absent Duke, they believe, has gone abroad to take part in peace talks with neighbouring states.

The conversation soon drifts to more earthy matters; and as they talk flippantly about venereal diseases and their effects, the owner of the local brothel, Mistress Overdone, appears.

Lucio complains that he has spent a fortune at her establishment and suffered from several bouts of disease as a result. The three men continue to joke about the consequences of their sexual antics, but their mood changes suddenly when they hear some grim news about their friend Claudio:

> *Mistress Overdone:* ... There's one yonder arrested and carried to prison, was worth five thousand of you all.
> *Gentleman:* Who's that, I prithee?
> *Mistress Overdone:* Marry sir, that's Claudio; Signior Claudio.
> *Gentleman:* Claudio to prison? 'Tis not so.
> *Mistress Overdone:* Nay, but I know 'tis so. I saw him arrested: saw him carried away: and which is more, within these three days his head to be chopped off.
> *Lucio:* But, after all this fooling, I would not have it so. Art thou sure of this?
> *Mistress Overdone:* I am too sure of it: and it is for getting Madam Julietta with child.

The men are shocked; there has been talk recently of harsher penalties for immorality, and it seems that Claudio is a victim of the new policy. They set off to find out what has happened. As they leave, Mistress Overdone reflects sadly on the state of her business. Times are hard for a brothel-keeper:

> *Mistress Overdone:* Thus, what with the war, what with the sweat,[1] what with the gallows, and what with poverty, I am custom-shrunk.[2]
>
> [1] *sweating sickness; plague*
> [2] *I have very few customers*

Mistress Overdone's servant Pompey Bum now approaches. He has just heard a public decree, and it does not bode well for either of them:

> *Pompey:* You have not heard of the proclamation, have you?
> *Mistress Overdone:* What proclamation, man?
> *Pompey:* All houses[1] in the suburbs of Vienna must be plucked down.
>
> [1] *bawdy houses, brothels*

In short, all the brothels outside the city centre, like Mistress Overdone's, are to be demolished. Pompey tries to console his mistress, who is distraught at the news. One way or another, he reassures her, they will manage to carry on their trade. Hearing a sudden uproar nearby, the two of them decide to make themselves scarce.

> *... what with the war, what with the sweat, what with the gallows ...*
>
> Mistress Overdone's list of grievances would have struck a chord with Shakespeare's audience. Only a matter of months before the first performances of *Measure for Measure*, there had been anxiety over the continuing war with Spain; a virulent outbreak of the plague had swept through London, leaving the streets deserted; and a plot to overthrow the new king had been uncovered, resulting in numerous executions. Pompey's news, too, would have had contemporary echoes:
>
> "*Measure for Measure begins from an attempt by the authorities to cleanse a city of licentiousness. In the period from May to December 1603, when the theatres were closed due to the worst outbreak of plague for a decade, a royal proclamation ordered a programme of slum clearance in the 'suburbs' such as Southwark, as an attempt simultaneously to prevent the spread of infection between closely packed dwellings and to get rid of brothels and ale-houses full of idle, indigent, dissolute and dangerous people.*"
>
> Jonathan Bate, *Soul of the Age*, 2008

The condemned man

The source of the commotion now becomes clear. Claudio has been arrested, just as Mistress Overdone had said: and the provost – who is in charge of the city's prison – is parading him through the city streets. Officers of the law are accompanying him, and Lucio and his friends are crowding round.

Claudio is dismayed that he should be put on public display in this way, and is anxious to get to the privacy of his prison cell. The provost explains that he is acting on the orders of the new ruler of Vienna:

> *Claudio:* Fellow, why dost thou show me thus to th'world?
> Bear me to prison, where I am committed.
> *Provost:* I do it not in evil disposition,[1]
> But from Lord Angelo by special charge.[2]
>
> [1] *from malice*
> [2] *specific instruction*

Claudio tells his friend that following his own pleasure has led to his downfall:

> *Lucio:* Whence comes this restraint?[1]
> *Claudio:* From too much liberty,[2] my Lucio.
> ... Our natures do pursue,
> Like rats that ravin down their proper bane,[3]
> A thirsty evil; and when we drink, we die.
>
> [1] *arrest, captivity*
> [2] *self-indulgence*
> [3] *that greedily devour the very poison that will kill them*

Claudio explains that he and Juliet were engaged to be married. They had not yet broken the news of their plans to Juliet's relatives, who were in charge of her dowry; as soon as they had done that, and received her family's approval, they planned to go ahead with the wedding ceremony. In the meantime, Juliet had fallen pregnant, a fact that is now only too obvious.

It appears that the Duke's new deputy, Angelo, has decided to make his mark by enforcing old, neglected laws against sexual misconduct. As a result, Claudio is facing the death penalty:

Claudio: ... this new governor
Awakes me all the enrolled penalties[1]
Which have, like unscour'd[2] armour, hung by th'wall
So long, that nineteen zodiacs have gone round,
And none of them been worn; and for a name
Now puts the drowsy and neglected act
Freshly on me[3] ...

[1] *revives all the official punishments that apply to my case*
[2] *rusty, unused*
[3] *to enhance his reputation, penalises me with long-forgotten laws*

Claudio believes that his only hope lies with his sister Isabella, who is about to enter a convent. He is sure that her charm and eloquence will move Angelo and persuade him to take a less drastic attitude:

Claudio: ... Implore her, in my voice,[1] that she make friends
To the strict deputy: bid herself assay[2] him.
I have great hope in that. For in her youth
There is a prone and speechless dialect[3]
Such as move men; beside, she hath prosperous art
When she will play with reason and discourse,
And well she can persuade.

[1] *in my name, on my behalf*
[2] *try to influence*
[3] *meek, quiet manner*

Lucio agrees to talk to Isabella at once. He hopes that she will succeed, and not only for Claudio's sake; after all, if sexual indiscretions are to be punished so severely, they are all in danger.

Claudio's death sentence would have seemed just as shocking to Shakespeare's original audiences, hardened as they were to severe punishments, as it does to us.

Sexual relations between a couple who had made a verbal agreement to marry were not necessarily considered an offence, as long as a formal marriage ceremony followed in due course. Shakespeare and Anne Hathaway had found themselves in this predicament in the autumn of 1582; a marriage was hastily arranged, eventually taking place three months into Anne's pregnancy.

"The audiences for whom Shakespeare wrote Measure for Measure *were used to seeing punishments inflicted on offenders against the law. In major towns and cities, executions were public entertainments. The pillory and the stocks were used to display and humiliate criminals. Whippings for certain offences, including sexual misdemeanours, were commonplace and were public ...*

"Yet the Vienna of Measure for Measure *is not early 17th-century England, even if its lowlife scenes might as well be set in London. While sexual incontinence was denounced by Christian moralists in Shakespeare's England, there was no such law as that by which Claudio is sentenced to death ... In Shakespeare's day it was conventional for a couple to take each other as man and wife well before the confirmation of a church ceremony. Such a private, sexually consummated, agreement had legal force. We should not assume that the first audiences of* Measure for Measure *would have been less forgiving of Claudio than we might be."*

    John Mullan, Measure for Measure *and Punishment*, 2016

An undercover mission   I, iii

The Duke has come to a monastery, and is visiting a friar in his cell. He has just asked the friar to shelter him secretly in the monastery while he is away from the Viennese court. He brushes aside the friar's suggestion that the Duke may be embarking on a secret love affair; something much more important is at stake.

Before leaving the court and handing power to his deputy Angelo, the Duke explains, he announced that he was travelling to Poland. The real reason for his departure, he reveals, was very different. What lay behind the Duke's decision was his concern about the lax state of the law in Vienna. For years, many of the city's strictest decrees have been ignored. Although they still exist, they have not been enforced, and the law is in danger of becoming a laughing stock.

Like children who know they will escape punishment, the citizens of Vienna are becoming unruly:

> *Duke:* ... Now, as fond fathers,
> Having bound up the threatening twigs of birch,
> Only to stick it in their children's sight
> For terror, not to use, in time the rod [1]
> Becomes more mock'd than fear'd: so our decrees,
> Dead to infliction, to themselves are dead,[2]
> And Liberty plucks Justice by the nose ...
>
> [1] *cane, birch*
> [2] *since they are no longer implemented, are as good as dead*

The friar asks the Duke why he has not chosen to apply the law more strictly himself, rather than assign the task to Angelo. He replies that it would be unjust if he, who had tacitly allowed immoral behaviour to flourish, were suddenly to start punishing it severely. Instead, he has decided to entrust the work to a deputy.

In the meantime, the Duke himself intends to remain in Vienna to observe the operation of the new regime. This is why he has come to the monastery; he wishes to disguise himself as a friar so that he can blend in unnoticed as he wanders around the city. In this, he will need the monastery's assistance:

> *Duke:* ... to behold his sway,[1]
> I will, as 'twere a brother of your order,[2]
> Visit both prince and people. Therefore, I prithee,
> Supply me with the habit,[3] and instruct me
> How I may formally in person bear[4]
> Like a true friar.
>
> [1] *to observe Angelo's rule*
> [2] *as if I were a member of your monastic community*
> [3] *friar's clothing*
> [4] *how I should conduct myself*

There is another thing that the Duke wishes to observe. Angelo prides himself on his strict, puritanical approach to life. Will the possession of power reveal a different side to his character?

> *Duke:* Lord Angelo is precise;[1]
> Stands at a guard with Envy;[2] scarce confesses
> That his blood flows; or that his appetite
> Is more to bread than stone. Hence shall we see
> If power change purpose, what our seemers be.[3]
>
> [1] *austere, inflexible*
> [2] *is constantly on guard against malice*
> [3] *if power can change a person's principles, the contrast between Angelo's public face and his true nature will be exposed*

Lord Angelo is precise ...

When King James came to the throne, religion was still a divisive issue, as it had been since Henry VIII had separated the English Church from Rome seventy years before. In particular, the new king was under pressure from the Puritans, radical Protestants who believed that the Church of England should rid itself completely of all forms of Catholic ritual.

James favoured tolerance in religious matters and intensely disliked the Puritans, regarding them as dogmatic and overzealous, a view almost certainly shared by Shakespeare:

"The first years of James's reign were marked by a profounder questioning, but also by more explicit affirmations, than Elizabethan times; and the need to hold on firmly to a middle way in the church, the state, and in private life was repeatedly stressed by the king himself. In this climate of ideas the mixed form of tragicomedy, exploring the double process of conflict and conciliation, would prove morally and aesthetically satisfying."

J. W. Lever, Introduction to the Arden edition of *Measure for Measure*, 1965

Disturbing news for Isabella   I, iv

Claudio's sister Isabella is shortly to become a nun. She is at the convent now, talking to Sister Francisca about the religious life. They are interrupted by a sudden shout at the door. It is a man's voice. Francisca, according to the rules of her order, cannot speak to a man except in the presence of the prioress, so she leaves Isabella to receive the caller.

The visitor is Lucio. He has come, as requested by Claudio, to ask for Isabella's help. She knows nothing of the trouble he is in, and is shocked to hear that her brother is in prison and his fiancée is pregnant. She asks why Claudio cannot marry Juliet to resolve the situation.

Unfortunately things are not as simple as that, Lucio replies. Vienna has a new ruler, an ascetic, uncompromising individual:

> Lucio: The Duke is very strangely[1] gone from hence ...
> Upon his place,
> And with full line of his authority,
> Governs Lord Angelo; a man whose blood
> Is very snow-broth;[2] one who never feels
> The wanton stings and motions of the sense;[3]
> But doth rebate and blunt his natural edge
> With profits of the mind, study and fast.[4]
>
> [1] *unaccountably, for no clear reason*
> [2] *is as cold and thin as melting snow*
> [3] *uncontrollable urges and sensual desires*
> [4] *deadens the natural keenness of his impulses with worthy intellectual pursuits and fasting*

The Duke's deputy is now restoring the draconian old laws against immorality, long ignored by the citizens of Vienna, and intends to make an example of Claudio:

> Lucio: He, to give fear to use and liberty,[1]
> Which have for long run by the hideous law
> As mice by lions,[2] hath pick'd out an act
> Under whose heavy sense your brother's life
> Falls into forfeit[3] ...
>
> [1] *to intimidate people who have become accustomed to unrestrained freedom*
> [2] *who have disregarded the fearsome law, like mice running past a sleeping lion*
> [3] *has chosen to reintroduce a law under which your brother faces the death penalty*

If Angelo persists in following the letter of the law, Claudio will be executed. Isabella is horrified, but feels powerless to help. Lucio urges her to visit Angelo and try to change his mind:

> Lucio: ... as I hear, the Provost hath a warrant
> For his execution.

Isabella: Alas, what poor ability's in me
To do him good!
Lucio: Assay[1] the power you have.
Isabella: My power? Alas, I doubt.
Lucio: Our doubts are traitors,
And make us lose the good we oft might win
By fearing to attempt.

[1] *try, put to the test*

Eventually Isabella agrees: she will go to Angelo and plead for her brother's life. Lucio urges her to act as soon as possible. There is no time to lose.

Two views of justice II, i

Angelo and Escalus, his second in command, are in a courtroom discussing legal matters. The law must be applied aggressively, argues Angelo. If this does not happen, it will lose its power to intimidate wrongdoers:

Angelo: We must not make a scarecrow of the law,
Setting it up to fear[1] the birds of prey,
And let it keep one shape[2] till custom make it
Their perch, and not their terror.

[1] *frighten*
[2] *let it remain unchanged*

Escalus is unsure. He feels that the law should be used prudently, dealing with offences like a scalpel rather than a heavy, blunt instrument. He is particularly concerned about the sentence passed on Claudio, which he considers excessive. He mentions that he knew the young man's father:

Escalus: … Let us be keen,[1] and rather cut a little,
Than fall,[2] and bruise to death. Alas, this gentleman,
Whom I would save, had a most noble father.

[1] *sharp, shrewd*
[2] *cause to fall, chop down*

Escalus gently suggests that Angelo himself may have been guilty, at some time in his life, of the kind of sexual indiscretion for which Claudio is facing execution. Angelo brushes the point aside. Even if it were true, the principles of justice remain the same, regardless of any wrongdoing committed by individuals involved in the legal process. Courts must make impartial decisions on the cases put before them:

> *Angelo:* 'Tis one thing to be tempted, Escalus,
> Another thing to fall. I not deny
> The jury passing[1] on the prisoner's life
> May in the sworn twelve[2] have a thief, or two,
> Guiltier than him they try. What's open made to justice,
> That justice seizes.[3]
>
> [1] *passing sentence, giving their verdict*
> [2] *included in the twelve members of the jury*
> [3] *justice operates on whatever situations are presented to it*

If Angelo were to be found guilty of a similar offence himself, he insists, he would expect the same penalty. There can be no compromise. He calls for Claudio's jailer, and orders him to carry out the sentence. Escalus reflects that, regardless of justice, the world is an imperfect place. All anyone can hope for is divine mercy:

> *Angelo:*   Sir, he must die.
> *Escalus:* Be it as your wisdom will.[1]
> *Angelo:*   Where is the Provost?
> *Provost:* Here, if it like your honour.
> *Angelo:*   See that Claudio
> Be executed by nine tomorrow morning;
> Bring him his confessor, let him be prepar'd,
> For that's the utmost of his pilgrimage.[2]
> *Escalus:* Well, heaven forgive him; and forgive us all.
> Some rise by sin, and some by virtue fall.[3]
>
> [1] *wishes, decrees*
> [2] *the end of his earthly journey*
> [3] *some people prosper by doing evil, and some are brought down by their good deeds*

A caution for Pompey

Elbow, a constable, has arrested two men and brought them to the courtroom. One is Pompey, Mistress Overdone's servant, and the other is Froth, a customer at her brothel.

Elbow attempts to explain why he has detained the two men, but his command of language is so haphazard that Angelo and Escalus can scarcely understand what crime has been committed:

Elbow: ... I do lean upon[1] justice, sir, and do bring in here before your good honour two notorious benefactors.
Angelo: Benefactors? Well, what benefactors are they? Are they not malefactors?
Elbow: If it please your honour, I know not well what they are. But precise[2] villains they are, that I am sure of, and void of all profanation in the world ...

[1] *I'm supported by, I'm relying on*
[2] *absolute, definite*

Eventually it emerges that Mistress Overdone, whose premises were demolished under Angelo's campaign against vice, has opened a new brothel masquerading as a bath-house.

Elbow insists that his pregnant wife was insulted by Pompey and Froth while she was innocently visiting the bath-house, but the facts of the case are lost in Elbow's baffling accusations and Pompey's lengthy, rambling descriptions.

Angelo loses patience with the pair, and leaves the courtroom. Escalus perseveres with his questions. Unable to establish what Froth has done wrong, he instructs the constable to release the man until his crime becomes clear:

>*Elbow:* ... What is't your worship's pleasure I shall do with this wicked caitiff?[1]
>
>*Escalus:* Truly, officer, because he hath some offences in him that thou wouldst discover if thou couldst, let him continue in his courses[2] till thou know'st what they are.
>
>[1] *villain, wretch*
>[2] *carry on behaving in the same way*

Elbow, interpreting this as a punishment of some kind, is delighted. Froth leaves, and Escalus turns to Pompey. He has no illusions about the man's business, he declares. Pompey argues that he is just trying to make a living:

>*Escalus:* Pompey, you are partly a bawd,[1] Pompey, howsoever you colour it in being a tapster,[2] are you not? Come, tell me true, it shall be the better for you.
>
>*Pompey:* Truly, sir, I am a poor fellow that would live.
>
>*Escalus:* How would you live, Pompey? By being a bawd? What do you think of the trade, Pompey? Is it a lawful trade?
>
>*Pompey:* If the law would allow it, sir.
>
>*Escalus:* But the law will not allow it, Pompey ...
>
>[1] *pimp*
>[2] *however hard you try to disguise your occupation by serving drinks*

> "*Angelo despises the people before him so much that he can't bother to listen to their meanderings. The phrase 'Judge not, that ye be not judged,' comes to mind. What it surely means, among other things, is: If you despise other people for their moral inferiority to yourself, your own superiority won't last long; in fact, it's effectively disappeared already.*"
>
> Northrop Frye, *On Shakespeare*, 1986

Prostitution is a fact of life, claims Pompey; the authorities will never be able to stop it as long as people have sexual desires. Escalus warns of the severe penalties that are planned for prostitutes and their clients, but Pompey is unmoved:

Pompey: Does your worship mean to geld and splay [1] all the youth of the city? ... If your worship will take orders for the drabs and the knaves,[2] you need not to fear the bawds.

Escalus: There is pretty orders beginning, I can tell you. It is but heading [3] and hanging.

Pompey: If you head and hang all that offend that way but for ten year together, you'll be glad to give out a commission for more heads [4] ...

[1] *sterilise*
[2] *arrange for this to happen to all the wanton young women and men*
[3] *beheading*
[4] *issue a request for more people, in order to repopulate the city*

Escalus repeats his warning that harsh punishments will be handed out to those involved in prostitution. If Pompey offends again, he will be in serious trouble. Pompey thanks Escalus for his advice. As he leaves, however, he makes it clear that he has no intention of changing his ways:

> *Pompey:* I thank your worship for your good counsel;
> [*aside*] but I shall follow it as the flesh and
> fortune shall better determine.[1]
>
> [1] *whether I follow it or not will be determined by my own feelings and circumstances*

Now that the two detainees have been released, Escalus turns to Elbow. When he learns that the constable has been in his job for over seven years, he tactfully suggests that it might be time for someone else to take on the role. There are very few candidates with his aptitude and intelligence, explains Elbow: in any case, when others have been chosen, they have willingly paid Elbow to do the job in their place. Escalus, keen to find someone more competent, asks him to prepare a list of possible recruits.

Finally, Escalus addresses the official who has remained in the courtroom. It is clear that the death sentence passed on Claudio is still troubling him. However, he can see no alternative: once a decision has been made, it must be carried out. Showing leniency, he tells himself, would only create further problems:

> *Escalus:* It grieves me for the death of Claudio,
> But there's no remedy.
> *Justice:* Lord Angelo is severe.
> *Escalus:* It is but needful.[1]
> Mercy is not itself, that oft looks so;[2]
> Pardon is still the nurse of second woe.[3]
> But yet, poor Claudio!
>
> [1] *his severity is no more than the circumstances require*
> [2] *what appears merciful may not always be so*
> [3] *pardoning a crime always leads to more suffering*

An unsettling encounter II, ii

The provost has come to see Angelo, hoping that he may have changed his mind about Claudio's execution. Angelo dismisses his concerns impatiently:

Provost: Is it your will Claudio shall die tomorrow?
Angelo: Did I not tell thee yea? Hadst thou not order?
Why dost thou ask again?
Provost: Lest I might be too rash.
Under your good correction,[1] I have seen
When, after execution, judgement hath
Repented o'er his doom.[2]
Angelo: Go to; let that be mine;[3]
Do you your office,[4] or give up your place ...

[1] *if you will excuse my saying so*
[2] *the judge has regretted the sentence that he inflicted*
[3] *drop the subject; that's my responsibility*
[4] *carry out your duty, stick to your job*

It would be easy to find someone to take his place, Angelo suggests. The provost, apologising, mentions that there is one further consideration: Juliet, Claudio's pregnant fiancée, is due to give birth very soon. Angelo tells him to make sure that she is secretly hurried away to a suitable place, and provided with any necessities.

A visitor now arrives. She humbly requests Angelo's attention, explaining that she is Isabella, the condemned man's sister. Claudio's friend Lucio has come with her to lend his support.

25

Isabella hates the immorality that has led to her brother's predicament, but asks Angelo to distinguish the sin from the sinner, and to show leniency. The provost fervently agrees. However, Angelo declares that the notion is absurd. The purpose of justice is to punish wrongdoers, not simply to state what is right and what is wrong:

Isabella: I have a brother is condemn'd to die;
I do beseech you, let it be his fault,[1]
And not my brother.
Provost: [*aside*] Heaven give thee moving graces!
Angelo: Condemn the fault, and not the actor of it?
Why, every fault's condemn'd ere it be done:[2]
Mine were the very cipher of a function
To fine the faults, whose fine stands in record,[3]
And let go by the actor.[4]
Isabella: O just but severe law!

[1] *let the fault be condemned*
[2] *every crime, by definition, is judged to be wrong before it is even committed*
[3] *my role would be meaningless if I were simply to criticise those actions that are already forbidden by law*
[4] *allow the perpetrator to go unpunished*

Isabella unhappily accepts the argument, and prepares to leave. However, Lucio urges her not to give up so easily. She must be more demonstrative and passionate, he insists, and she turns to Angelo again. Surely it lies within his power, she asks, to show mercy? The law is the law, he replies, and must be enforced.

Encouraged by Lucio, Isabella continues on the theme of mercy. God himself, who is all-powerful, does not sentence us all to damnation for our sins, but shows forgiveness; what would happen to Angelo if God showed him no mercy? Passing judgement is not a matter of his personal feelings, responds Angelo:

Isabella: How would you be
If He, which is the top of judgement,[1] should
But judge you as you are? O, think on that …

Angelo: Be you content, fair maid;
It is the law, not I, condemn your brother;
Were he my kinsman, brother, or my son,
It should be thus with him. He must die tomorrow.

[1] *God, who is our ultimate judge*

Isabella raises another argument: her brother's offence is far from unusual, but she has never before heard that it was punishable by death. That is because the existing law has not been properly applied, says Angelo. Punishing first offences to the full will prevent future wickedness, and in this sense shows true compassion for humanity in general:

Isabella: Good, good my lord, bethink you: [1]
Who is it that hath died for this offence?
There's many have committed it.
Lucio: [*aside*] Ay, well said.
Angelo: The law hath not been dead, though it hath slept:
Those many had not dar'd to do that evil
If the first that did th'edict infringe
Had answer'd for his deed. [2] Now 'tis awake ...
Isabella: Yet show some pity.
Angelo: I show it most of all when I show justice ...

[1] *consider this*
[2] *none of those earlier offenders would have dared to commit fornication if the first of them had paid the price for his actions*

There is a difference between genuine leadership and petty tyranny, insists Isabella; in a wise ruler, power is tempered by sympathy and self-awareness. If Angelo can find within himself any trace of the flaw for which Claudio stands condemned, he should think again.

Angelo, while remaining outwardly unmoved, is deeply affected by Isabella's words:

> *Isabella:* ... authority, though it err like others,
> Hath yet a kind of medicine in itself
> That skins the vice o'th'top.[1] Go to your bosom,
> Knock there, and ask your heart what it doth know
> That's like my brother's fault. If it confess
> A natural guiltiness, such as is his,
> Let it not sound a thought upon your tongue
> Against my brother's life.
> *Angelo:* [*aside*] She speaks, and 'tis such sense
> That my sense breeds with it.[2]
>
> [1] *those in authority, though they have faults like everyone else, find a way of covering up their failings without curing them*
> [2] *she speaks with such wisdom that my feelings are roused*

Finally Angelo agrees to meet Isabella again tomorrow, and he prepares to leave. Lucio is horrified when Isabella suddenly makes an offer to bribe Angelo. However, it immediately becomes clear that, in her innocence, she is offering to pray on the deputy's behalf:

> *Angelo:* I will bethink me.[1] [*Leaving*] Come again tomorrow.
> *Isabella:* Hark, how I'll bribe you: good my lord, turn back.
> *Angelo:* How! Bribe me?
> *Isabella:* Ay, with such gifts that heaven shall share with you.
> *Lucio:* [*aside*] You had marr'd all else.[2]
> *Isabella:* Not with fond sickles of the tested gold[3] ...
> ... but with true prayers,
> That shall be up at heaven and enter there
> Ere sunrise ...
>
> [1] *I will consider what you have said*
> [2] *all your good work would have been ruined if you hadn't made that clear*
> [3] *not with coins of pure gold, which some people foolishly prize*

... authority, though it err like others ...

It is not known whether *Measure for Measure* was a popular play in its time. The king's Master of the Revels records that it was performed at Court in December 1604, and it had probably been staged at the Globe Theatre during the summer of that year; however, nothing more is heard of the play during Shakespeare's lifetime.

Fifty years after Shakespeare's death, an unsuccessful attempt was made to adapt the play to the changing tastes of the time: the bawdy characters were removed, music and dancing were added, and, bizarrely, the central characters from another play, *Much Ado About Nothing*, were incorporated.

Eventually the original play was revived, but during the 18th and 19th centuries it was generally regarded as undignified and problematic, and was usually abridged to some extent. It was not until the 20th century that the drama in its full, authentic form emerged once more:

"It is little wonder that the play of Shakespeare's in which the word 'authority' occurs more often than in any other should have an extraordinary pertinence for a century in which the word 'authoritarian' is on so many lips."

Harold C. Goddard, *The Meaning of Shakespeare*, 1951

It is time to leave, Lucio tells Isabella: she has done all she can, and seems to have made an impression on Angelo. The two of them depart, and Angelo remains alone with his thoughts.

It immediately becomes clear that Isabella has, without realising it, aroused deep, lustful feelings in Angelo. He is shocked and ashamed, particularly as her obvious virtue and modesty make him desire her all the more. The blame clearly lies with him, not with her:

> *Angelo:* What's this? What's this? Is this her fault, or mine?
> The tempter, or the tempted, who sins most, ha?
> Not she; nor doth she tempt; but it is I
> That, lying by the violet in the sun,
> Do as the carrion does, not as the flower,
> Corrupt with virtuous season.[1]
>
> [1] *the radiant goodness that makes her flourish brings out the moral corruption in me, as if I were a piece of flesh rotting in the sun*

Acutely aware of his own hypocrisy, Angelo agonises over his illicit desires. He has never felt this way about a woman before:

> *Angelo:* Never could the strumpet
> With all her double vigour, art and nature,[1]
> Once stir my temper:[2] but this virtuous maid
> Subdues me quite.[3] Ever till now
> When men were fond,[4] I smil'd, and wonder'd how.
>
> [1] *with the twofold power of her seductive skills and her natural attractiveness*
> [2] *disturb my self-control*
> [3] *has completely overpowered me*
> [4] *infatuated, besotted*

Juliet's anguish II, iii

Duke Vincentio, disguised in the heavy, hooded cloak of a friar, has come to the prison where Claudio is spending the night before his execution. He asks the provost to allow him to visit some of the inmates so that he can offer comfort to them.

As they are talking, the pregnant Juliet approaches: the provost, as instructed by Angelo, has taken responsibility for her welfare. He remarks that Claudio, rather than being punished, should be encouraged to marry her and produce more offspring:

> *Provost:* She is with child,
> And he that got[1] it, sentenc'd: a young man
> More fit to do another such offence,[2]
> Than die for this.
>
> [1] *fathered*
> [2] *who should rightly have more children*

The Duke questions Juliet, and it immediately becomes clear that, although she regrets her misdeed, she loves Claudio, and their desire for each other was mutual. Satisfied that she is truly repentant, the Duke leaves to visit Claudio.

Juliet, whose pregnancy means that her life has been spared, is distraught at being reminded that her loved one is to die:

> *Duke:* Your partner, as I hear, must die tomorrow,
> And I am going with instruction[1] to him.
> Grace go with you: *Benedicite.*[2]
> *Juliet:* Must die tomorrow! O injurious love,
> That respites me a life, whose very comfort
> Is still a dying horror![3]
>
> [1] *advice, spiritual guidance*
> [2] *God bless you*
> [3] *whose consequences have saved my life whilst forcing me to live with the horror of Claudio's death*

Angelo's proposition II, iv

Still agitated, Angelo reflects that, in his distraction, he is unable to pray. His words may be directed to heaven, but his thoughts are dominated by his lust for Isabella.

Everything else now seems meaningless. Matters of state and government, which were previously so important to him, now seem dry and tedious. His own solemn and dignified demeanour, which he has deliberately and proudly promoted, now seems worthless; as a ruler, he might just as well strut around arrogantly. The fact that he holds authority shows how easily people are deceived:

> *Angelo:* O place,[1] O form,[2]
> How often dost thou with thy case, thy habit,[3]
> Wrench awe from fools, and tie the wiser souls
> To thy false seeming![4]

[1] *status, high office*
[2] *ceremony, formality*
[3] *outward appearance*
[4] *inspire awe in foolish people, and ensnare even wiser people with your superficial appeal*

When a servant announces that Isabella has returned, Angelo struggles to contain his emotions. When she comes in, he manages to remain calm, and tells her again that Claudio must die. However, on realising that she is prepared to accept his verdict and leave, he hints that Claudio's life may be spared, at least temporarily:

> *Angelo:* ... Your brother cannot live.
> *Isabella:* Even so.[1] Heaven keep your honour.
> *Angelo:* Yet may he live a while; and, it may be,
> As long as you or I; yet he must die.

[1] *as I feared*

Assuming that Angelo has only a short reprieve in mind, Isabella asks when the execution will take place, so that Claudio can prepare his soul for death. Angelo now changes his tone suddenly, and declares that Claudio's crime cannot be pardoned. Creating a new life unlawfully is as bad as taking a life, he argues. Isabella replies that, even if this is the law of heaven, people on earth do not regard the two sins as equal.

Angelo questions Isabella as to whether, theoretically, wrongdoing might be acceptable if Claudio's life were saved as a result:

> *Angelo:*   Answer to this:
> I – now the voice of the recorded law [1] –
> Pronounce a sentence on your brother's life:
> Might there not be a charity in sin [2]
> To save this brother's life?
>
> > [1] *as a spokesman for the established law, not expressing my own opinion*
> > [2] *might it not be compassionate to commit a sin*

Isabella agrees enthusiastically, imagining that the sin Angelo has in mind is to pardon Claudio rather than apply the letter of the law. If leniency is a fault, she will gladly take full responsibility, both for her requesting it and for his granting it. Angelo, becoming impatient, accuses her of wilfully misunderstanding him:

> *Isabella:* That I do beg his life, if it be sin,
>   Heaven let me bear it; [1] you granting of my suit,
>   If that be sin, I'll make it my morn prayer
>   To have it added to the faults of mine,
>   And nothing of your answer. [2]
> *Angelo:*   Nay, but hear me;
>   Your sense pursues not mine: [3] either you are ignorant,
>   Or seem so, crafty; [4] and that's not good.
>
> > [1] *be blamed for it*
> > [2] *something for which you need take no responsibility*
> > [3] *you are not following my meaning*
> > [4] *or you are craftily pretending not to understand*

Angelo tries a more direct approach. He poses a question, claiming to speak hypothetically: if the only way of saving her brother's life were to lose her virginity to someone with the power to pardon him, what would she do? Isabella replies without hesitation that she would die rather than yield up her body against her will.

Angelo reminds her that this would mean her brother's death, but she is adamant:

> *Isabella:* Better it were a brother died at once,
> Than that a sister, by redeeming him,
> Should die for ever.

Changing his line of argument yet again, Angelo suggests that Isabella does not take the law, and Claudio's offence, seriously. She apologises: the sin of fornication is abhorrent to her, but she may have trivialised it when defending her brother.

Human beings are frail and susceptible to temptation, replies Angelo, both men and women. Isabella agrees; all too often, women allow themselves to be influenced and exploited by men. If frailty is natural, Angelo urges, then Isabella should not be afraid to show her vulnerability.

To Isabella's distress, Angelo now advances on her passionately. She hopes, desperately, that he is deliberately playing a provocative role, and does not mean what he says:

> *Angelo:* Plainly conceive,[1] I love you.
> *Isabella:* My brother did love Juliet,
> And you tell me that he shall die for't.
> *Angelo:* He shall not, Isabel, if you give me love.
> *Isabella:* I know your virtue hath a licence in't,
> Which seems a little fouler than it is,
> To pluck on others.[2]
>
> [1] *understand*
> [2] *a virtuous judge is allowed to say things that seem improper in order to test other people's responses*

When it becomes obvious that Angelo is serious, Isabella, furious at his hypocrisy, throws his words back at him:

Angelo: Believe me, on mine honour,
My words express my purpose.
Isabella: Ha? Little honour, to be much believ'd,[1]
And most pernicious purpose! Seeming,[2] seeming!

[1] *your own words show how little honour you have in reality*
[2] *deceit, pretence*

In her anger, Isabella threatens to denounce Angelo in public, revealing his duplicity, if he does not grant Claudio a reprieve at once. Angelo is unmoved:

Isabella: I will proclaim thee, Angelo, look for't.
Sign me a present[1] pardon for my brother,
Or with an outstretch'd throat I'll tell the world aloud
What man thou art.
Angelo: Who will believe thee, Isabel?

[1] *immediate*

Everything is in his favour, claims Angelo. He is renowned for his moral uprightness, and is considered a strict, even puritanical individual. If she makes her threatened allegations against him, she will be universally disbelieved and condemned for slander.

> *"Angelo is one of the clearest demonstrations in literature of the intoxicating nature of power. Power means unbounded opportunity, and opportunity acts on the criminal potentialities in man as gravitation does on an apple."*
>
> Harold C. Goddard, *The Meaning of Shakespeare*, 1951

Becoming increasingly roused and menacing, Angelo warns that, if Isabella fails to submit to his demands, Claudio will suffer a slow, painful death:

> *Angelo:* I have begun,
> And now I give my sensual race the rein: [1]
> Fit thy consent to my sharp appetite;
> Lay by all nicety and prolixious blushes [2]
> That banish what they sue for.[3] Redeem thy brother
> By yielding up thy body to my will;
> Or else he must not only die the death,
> But thy unkindness shall his death draw out
> To ling'ring sufferance.[4] Answer me tomorrow ...
>
> [1] *I'm giving free rein to my sensual desires*
> [2] *put aside all coyness and time-wasting protestations of innocence*
> [3] *drive away the reluctance that they pretend to encourage*
> [4] *prolonged suffering, torture*

Angelo storms out, leaving Isabella stunned and despondent. She knows that Angelo is right; no one will believe him capable of such corrupt behaviour. She resigns herself to losing her brother.

All that remains for her is to pay Claudio a final visit and tell him what has happened. Although his own crime was motivated by lust, he is a principled man, and will understand her rejection of Angelo's abhorrent offer. She will help him to prepare for his punishment:

> *Isabella:* Then, Isabel live chaste, and brother, die:
> More than our brother is our chastity.
> I'll tell him yet of Angelo's request,
> And fit his mind to death, for his soul's rest.

A friar's advice III, i

Claudio, in his prison cell, is talking to a friar, unaware that the man is in fact the Duke of Vienna in disguise. Claudio tells the friar that, while he hopes for Angelo's pardon, he is ready to die.

The Duke encourages him to commit fully to the acceptance of death. Life is transient and insignificant, he maintains, and must be seen for what it is, a futile struggle to avoid its own destiny:

Duke: Be absolute[1] for death: either death or life
Shall thereby be the sweeter. Reason[2] thus with life:
If I do lose thee, I do lose a thing
That none but fools would keep.
  ... thou art Death's fool;[3]
For him thou labour'st by thy flight to shun,
And yet run'st toward him still.[4]

[1] *resolved, positive*
[2] *talk, argue*
[3] *plaything, victim*
[4] *you toil constantly to try to avoid him, but are forever running towards him*

The qualities often attributed to life, such as nobility and courage, are illusory, as is the happiness that life supposedly brings:

Duke: Happy thou art not;
For what thou hast not, still thou striv'st to get,
And what thou hast, forget'st.[1]

[1] *you continually strive to possess the things you do not have, and fail to appreciate what you have*

Wealth, too, is a false aspiration, and provides no real comfort in old age. Despite all this, we cling on to life, even though death brings an end to all our uncertainties:

> *Duke:* ... when thou art old and rich,
> Thou hast neither heat, affection, limb, nor beauty
> To make thy riches pleasant.[1] What's yet in this
> That bears the name of life?[2] Yet in this life
> Lie hid moe thousand deaths;[3] yet death we fear
> That makes these odds all even.[4]
>
> [1] *you do not have the vitality, passion or strength to enjoy the riches you have saved*
> [2] *what is there in all this suffering that deserves to be called life?*
> [3] *there are a thousand other hidden woes*
> [4] *we still fear death, even though it eliminates all these difficulties*

A voice is heard outside the cell. The provost goes to investigate, and returns with Claudio's sister Isabella. The Duke takes his leave of Claudio, promising to return soon.

As the Duke is leaving, he takes the provost to one side. He wants to eavesdrop on the conversation between Claudio and his sister, he explains, and asks the provost to take him to a suitable hiding place.

A change of heart

Claudio asks Isabella if she has any comfort to offer him. His comfort will lie in heaven, she tells him gently. His execution will take place tomorrow, and he must be ready for his fate. She hints that a reprieve might be possible, but in circumstances that would be utterly intolerable. Claudio wants to know more:

> *Claudio:* Is there no remedy?
> *Isabella:* None, but such remedy as, to save a head,
> To cleave a heart in twain.[1]
> *Claudio:* But is there any?
> *Isabella:* Yes, brother, you may live;
> There is a devilish mercy in the judge,

If you'll implore it, that will free your life,
But fetter you² till death.

¹ *the only remedy, while it would prevent an execution, would break a heart in two*
² *keep you in chains*

Claudio persists: does she mean life imprisonment? In a sense, she replies; the only course that would save his life would result in permanent dishonour. Claudio, becoming increasingly impatient, demands to hear exactly what has been proposed.

Isabella, unwilling to say any more about her experience with Angelo, becomes defensive, and questions whether her brother is genuinely ready to face death. Although the prospect may be frightening, she assures him, the suffering is insignificant. Claudio, in turn, declares angrily that he is not afraid:

Isabella: Dar'st thou die?
The sense of death is most in apprehension; ¹
And the poor beetle that we tread upon
In corporal sufferance finds a pang as great
As when a giant dies.²
Claudio: Why give you me this shame?
Think you I can a resolution fetch
From flowery tenderness?³ If I must die,
I will encounter darkness as a bride
And hug it in mine arms.

¹ *the strongest feeling aroused by death is fearful anticipation*
² *in death, a giant suffers no more bodily pain than a beetle that we casually tread underfoot*
³ *do you think I need your clever, sympathetic words in order to summon my courage?*

Isabella is encouraged to hear that Claudio is so resolute; their father, now dead, would have approved. Claudio is clearly too noble to live a life of dishonour. She remarks how malicious and deceitful Angelo is, persecuting the city's youth even though he himself is deeply corrupt.

Claudio agrees, and Isabella now goes further. She reveals the appalling offer that Angelo has made to her. Claudio is shocked, and his first thought is that Isabella must reject his advances. She wishes it were her life rather than her virginity that was at stake:

> *Isabella:*   Dost thou think,[1] Claudio,
> If I would yield him my virginity
> Thou mightst be freed?
> *Claudio:*   O heavens, it cannot be!
> *Isabella:* Yes, he would give't thee, from this rank offence,
> So to offend him still.[2] This night's the time
> That I should do what I abhor to name;[3]
> Or else thou diest tomorrow.
> *Claudio:*   Thou shalt not do't.
> *Isabella:* O, were it but my life,
> I'd throw it down for your deliverance
> As frankly as a pin.[4]

> [1] *do you realise*
> [2] *through this vile offence, he would grant you the freedom to break the law again*
> [3] *I am supposed to do the deed that I cannot bear to name*
> [4] *if only he had demanded my life, I would give it up as freely as a pin in order to save you*

Claudio is astonished that Angelo should be so overcome by lust that he is prepared to make a mockery of the law. He reflects that lust is, perhaps, the least serious of the deadly sins: surely Angelo would not put his immortal soul at risk for a brief moment of pleasure?

The thought suddenly brings home the reality of Claudio's situation, and he is plunged into terror and despair:

Claudio: ... O Isabel!
Isabella: What says my brother?
Claudio: Death is a fearful thing.
Isabella: And shamed life a hateful.
Claudio: Ay, but to die, and go we know not where;
To lie in cold obstruction,[1] and to rot;
This sensible warm motion[2] to become
A kneaded clod[3] ...

[1] *rigidity, confinement*
[2] *this warm body, with its powers of feeling and movement*
[3] *a compressed lump of earth*

He imagines the terrible torments that await him: perhaps his spirit will be engulfed in flames, or locked in ice, or swept endlessly around the skies. Life, however painful and difficult it may be, must surely be preferable:

Claudio: The weariest and most loathed worldly life
That age, ache, penury and imprisonment
Can lay on nature,[1] is a paradise
To what we fear of death.[2]

[1] *inflict on our existence*
[2] *compared to our fearsome image of death*

41

Abandoning his earlier stoicism, Claudio suddenly begs his sister to change her mind. To submit to Angelo's desires would scarcely be a sin, he claims. Isabella is appalled:

> *Claudio:* Sweet sister, let me live.
> What [1] sin you do to save a brother's life,
> Nature dispenses with the deed so far [2]
> That it becomes a virtue.
> *Isabella:* O, you beast!
> O faithless coward! O dishonest wretch!
> Wilt thou be made a man [3] out of my vice?
>
> [1] *whatever*
> [2] *excuses the deed to such an extent*
> [3] *gain a new lease of life*

Claudio's request is utterly shameful, cries Isabella. He is unworthy even to be considered the true son of his father, she declares, and she will have nothing more to do with him. Even praying for his soul is out of the question.

Isabella refuses to let her brother say any more, accusing him of habitual wickedness. The wrongdoing that brought him to his prison cell was entirely intentional. To grant clemency would only encourage him to sin again:

> *Isabella:* Thy sin's not accidental, but a trade; [1]
> Mercy to thee would prove itself a bawd; [2]
> 'Tis best that thou diest quickly.
>
> [1] *a habit, a regular custom*
> [2] *would create more opportunities for illicit affairs*

With that, Isabella leaves, impervious to her brother's pleas.

> "*Angelo's opposite is Isabella, but many have noticed that she is also his twin – his fellow absolutist. She too has some extreme attitudes to punishment.*"
>
> John Mullan, Measure for Measure *and Punishment*, 2016

The Duke sees a way out

As Isabella is hurrying away, the Duke, coming out of his hiding place, stops her. He has something important to discuss with her, he says, and asks her to wait for a few minutes. He then goes into the cell to talk to Claudio.

Admitting to Claudio that he overheard the conversation that has just taken place, the Duke – who claims to be Angelo's personal confessor – casts a different light on Isabella's encounter with the deputy. He tells him that the offer to save Claudio's life was not genuine, but was a ruse to test Isabella's integrity. Angelo was, in fact, delighted to find that she was virtuous and incorruptible.

Whatever the outcome, then, there is no hope of a pardon. Claudio, exhausted and despondent, accepts his fate:

    Duke: Do not satisfy your resolution with hopes that are fallible;[1] tomorrow you must die; go to your knees, and make ready.
    Claudio: Let me ask my sister pardon; I am so out of love with life that I will sue[2] to be rid of it.

    [1] *do not take encouragement from false hopes*
    [2] *ask, plead*

As Claudio says farewell to his sister, the Duke speaks to the provost. He needs to be alone with Isabella, he explains; as a friar, he is completely trustworthy, and she is safe in his presence. The provost leaves, accompanying Claudio away from the cell.

43

The Duke immediately makes it clear that, despite his earlier remarks to Claudio, he knows the truth about Angelo's proposition: sadly, he reflects, such misconduct is not uncommon. The Duke also knows that Isabella is chaste and honourable, and asks her what she will do when she returns to Angelo to answer his demand.

Isabella is steadfast in her determination: she will refuse Angelo's advances. Unaware that she is speaking to the Duke himself, she reveals that she hopes one day to tell him the truth about Angelo:

> *Duke:* How will you do to content this substitute,[1] and to save your brother?
>
> *Isabella:* I am now going to resolve him.[2] I had rather my brother die by the law, than my son should be unlawfully born. But O, how much is the good Duke deceived in Angelo! If ever he return, and I can speak to him, I will open my lips in vain, or discover his government.[3]
>
> [1] *satisfy Angelo*
> [2] *leave him in no doubt*
> [3] *do everything that I can to reveal the truth about Angelo's conduct*

The Duke is sympathetic, but agrees with Isabella that Angelo would proclaim his innocence if publicly accused. However, he has a plan that may resolve the situation and bring a number of other benefits:

> *Duke:* … a remedy presents itself. I do make myself believe[1] that you may most uprighteously do a poor wronged lady a merited benefit; redeem your brother from the angry law; do no stain to your own gracious person; and much please the absent Duke, if peradventure he shall ever return to have hearing of this business.
>
> [1] *I am convinced*

Isabella is curious to know more, although she will not take part in anything dishonourable. The Duke explains that Angelo was once engaged to be married to a lady named Mariana. However, as the wedding-day approached, her brother was drowned in a shipwreck; and the money he was carrying, intended as Mariana's dowry to be presented to Angelo on their marriage, was lost with him.

Angelo's reaction was to withdraw from the marriage contract immediately, excusing his behaviour with false claims about his fiancée's reputation. To this day, Mariana is still grief-stricken:

Duke: ... she lost a noble and renowned brother, in his love toward her ever most kind and natural; with him, the portion and sinew [1] of her fortune, her marriage dowry; with both, her combinate [2] husband, this well-seeming Angelo.
Isabella: Can this be so? Did Angelo so leave her?
Duke: Left her in tears, and dried not one of them with his comfort: swallowed his vows whole, pretending in her discoveries of dishonour: [3] in few, bestowed her on her own lamentation, which she yet wears [4] for his sake ...

[1] *bulk*
[2] *committed, contracted*
[3] *claiming to have discovered evidence that she was dishonourable*
[4] *in short, left her with nothing but her own sorrow, which she continues to feel*

Isabella feels great sympathy for Mariana, who has been treated so cruelly by Angelo. She can do something to help, says the Duke; furthermore, she will save Claudio's life at the same time.

Despite everything, Mariana is still in love with Angelo, and hopes to marry him one day. The Duke proposes that Isabella should agree to Angelo's ultimatum, thereby saving her brother's life, as long as their sexual encounter takes place in darkness and silence.

45

When the time comes, however, it will be Mariana, not Isabella, who comes to Angelo's bed. There is every chance that, as a result, Angelo will be compelled to treat Mariana fairly:

> *Duke:* If the encounter acknowledge itself hereafter,[1] it may compel him to her recompense;[2] and here, by this, is your brother saved, your honour untainted, the poor Mariana advantaged, and the corrupt deputy scaled.[3]
>
> [1] *comes to light in the future*
> [2] *force him to make amends*
> [3] *weighed, subjected to moral judgement*

Isabella agrees to go along with the scheme. The Duke encourages her to keep her nerve when she meets Angelo; he then sets off at once to tell Mariana of his plan.

Shakespeare's plays have often been censored or amended, particularly where sexual or religious content is concerned. One clerical official decided that *Measure for Measure* was so problematic that all twenty-four pages of the text in his college's edition had to go:

"*The 17th-century censor at St Alban's, the Jesuit English College in Valladolid, Spain, clearly set to work to make their library copy of Shakespeare's collected works acceptable to seminarians. This largely took the form of excising unsuitable passages from the corpus of plays, and in particular, lines of bawdy humour and those which seemed to treat Catholic doctrine lightly ... Coming to* Measure for Measure, *Shakespeare's seedy story of sex and coercion and starring a novice nun and an ethically ambiguous disguised friar, however, no such piecemeal amelioration was possible. The twelve leaves have been summarily torn from the volume.*"

Laurie Maguire and Emma Smith, *30 Great Myths about Shakespeare*, 2013

A dubious reputation III, ii

In the streets outside the prison, the Duke is alarmed to witness a scene of commotion. Constable Elbow and his officers are dragging Pompey to the courtroom. The Duke reprimands Pompey for making his living from prostitution. Forgetting his disguise for a moment, he orders the constable to put him in prison. Elbow replies that his fate will be decided by Angelo, who has already issued Pompey with a warning:

> *Duke:* Take him to prison, officer:
> Correction and instruction[1] must both work
> Ere this rude beast will profit.
> *Elbow:* He must before the deputy,[2] sir; he has given him warning. The deputy cannot abide a whoremaster.
>
> [1] *punishment and education*
> [2] *he must be tried by Angelo*

Pompey is cheered to see Lucio passing by, confident that he will pay the bail required to keep him out of prison. Lucio, however, has no intention of helping him; in fact, he is amused at his friend's predicament, and teases him about his work at Mistress Overdone's brothel.

Pompey is taken away, and Lucio turns to the Duke. Believing that he is talking to a humble friar, Lucio remarks on the strict new regime that Angelo has introduced. It was wrong of the Duke to disappear so mysteriously, he feels:

> *Lucio:* It was a mad, fantastical trick of him to steal[1] from the state ... Lord Angelo dukes it well in his absence: he puts transgression to't.[2]
> *Duke:* He does well in't.
> *Lucio:* A little more lenity to lechery[3] would do no harm in him. Something too crabbed that way,[4] friar.
> *Duke:* It is too general a vice, and severity must cure it.
>
> [1] *abscond, slip away*
> [2] *he is tough on wrongdoing*
> [3] *tolerance towards lustful behaviour*
> [4] *he's rather too harsh in that respect*

47

Lucio agrees that debauchery is widespread, but believes that it will never be uprooted completely. He has heard rumours, he mentions, that Angelo was not conceived in the usual way, but produced by sea-creatures, and is in fact impotent.

Lucio then comes to the subject of Claudio and his imminent execution. The previous ruler would never have been so hard-hearted, he claims. He was known to be charitable, perhaps through his association with Vienna's low life. The Duke is taken aback to learn of his own reputation:

> *Lucio:* Why, what a ruthless thing is this in him, for the rebellion of a codpiece[1] to take away the life of a man! Would the Duke that is absent have done this? Ere[2] he would have hanged a man for the getting a hundred bastards, he would have paid for the nursing a thousand. He had some feeling of the sport;[3] he knew the service; and that instructed him to mercy.[4]
>
> *Duke:* I have never heard the absent Duke much detected for women;[5] he was not inclined that way.
>
> *Lucio:* O sir, you are deceived.
>
> *Duke:* 'Tis not possible.

> [1] *a sexual misdemeanour*
> [2] *before*
> [3] *appreciation for sensual pleasures*
> [4] *he was familiar with the sex industry, and that taught him to be tolerant*
> [5] *publicly accused of philandering*

Lucio boasts that he is a close friend of the Duke's; and although the ruler had a reputation for wisdom, Lucio knows better. He reveals that the Duke is a heavy drinker as well as a womaniser, and is far less enlightened than people realise.

Scarcely able to contain his indignation, the Duke scolds Lucio for spreading false, malicious gossip. If the absent Duke ever returns, he threatens, he will tell him of Lucio's slanders. Lucio insists that he has inside information; besides, he is not afraid of anything that a humble friar might say or do.

Complaining again of the new ruler's prudishness, and the injustice of Claudio's sentence, Lucio takes his leave.

Another victim

As the Duke broods over the perplexing rumours that he has just heard, another captive is hauled past him by officers of the law. This time it is Mistress Overdone who has been arrested. She is accompanied by Escalus and the provost, and her pleas for mercy are ignored. She is a notorious repeat offender:

> *Escalus:* Go, away with her to prison.
> *Mistress Overdone:* Good my lord, be good to me. Your honour is accounted a merciful man; good my lord.
> *Escalus:* Double and treble admonition, and still forfeit in the same kind![1] This would make mercy swear and play the tyrant.[2]
> *Provost:* A bawd of eleven years' continuance, may it please your honour.
>
> [1] *you have been warned several times, and you continue to offend in the same way*
> [2] *it's enough to make Mercy herself curse and resort to cruelty*

Mistress Overdone complains that Lucio has falsely informed on her. One of the prostitutes at her brothel, Kate Keepdown, has had Lucio's child: he agreed to marry her, but has not lived up to his promise. Mistress Overdone, in the meantime, has been looking after the child. Escalus decides to have the disreputable Lucio brought before him for questioning.

The officers of the law take Mistress Overdone away to prison. Escalus turns to the provost and discusses Claudio's case with him. He himself would not have been so severe with the young man, he remarks sadly, and asks the provost to ensure that Claudio has a spiritual adviser to help him in his final hours. The provost confirms that has been done; then, noticing the friar himself nearby, he introduces him to Escalus.

The disguised Duke tells Escalus that he is a visitor to Vienna, sent on a special religious mission from Rome. When Escalus asks if he brings any news from abroad, the Duke suggests, enigmatically, that the news is always the same, regardless of time or place:

> *Escalus:* What news abroad i'th'world?
> *Duke:* None, but that there is so great a fever on goodness that the dissolution of it must cure it.[1] Novelty is only in request,[2] and it is as dangerous to be aged in any kind of course as it is virtuous to be constant in any undertaking[3] ... This news is old enough, yet it is every day's news.
>
> [1] *virtue is in such a sorry condition that it can only be cured by its own death*
> [2] *people are only interested in the latest fashions*
> [3] *being consistent and principled is considered a danger, not a virtue*

The Duke then asks about his own reputation. Escalus remarks that he is an even-tempered, reflective man, not given to excitement or pleasure-seeking. However, for the moment Escalus is more concerned about Claudio than the Duke. He is glad to hear that, with the friar's help, the young man is resigned to his fate, and has given up his false hopes of a reprieve.

Once again, Escalus laments Angelo's rigorous application of the law in Claudio's case. The Duke remarks dryly that setting such high standards is not without its risks:

Escalus: I have laboured for the poor gentleman to the extremest shore of my modesty,[1] but my brother-justice have I found so severe that he hath forced me to tell him he is indeed Justice.[2]

Duke: If his own life answer the straitness of his proceeding,[3] it shall become him well: wherein if he chance to fail, he hath sentenced himself.[4]

[1] *the utmost that my subordinate position permits*
[2] *to acknowledge that he is Justice personified*
[3] *measures up to the strictness of his ruling*
[4] *if Angelo should fail to live up to his values, he will become a victim of his own severity*

Prostitution was widespread in the London of Shakespeare's time. It was tolerated as long as it remained confined to the suburbs; and the same was true of the public theatres, such as the Globe, which were hated by the Puritans who dominated the city authorities.

This uneasy compromise eventually broke down, and thirty years after Shakespeare's death the values embodied by the fictional Angelo gained, at least for a while, the upper hand:

"*Prostitution, like theatre, had rapidly expanded during Shakespeare's lifetime, catering to a demand generated by the increasing density of population in London ... Whorehouse and playhouse alike stood on the uncertain periphery of the city and the law: condemned but condoned, persecuted and permitted. The contradiction persisted until the outbreak of civil war: in 1642 the theatres were closed; in 1650 Parliament made unlawful fornication a crime, subject to three months' imprisonment, and adultery a felony, punishable by death.*"

Gary Taylor, *Reinventing Shakespeare*, 1990

A deception is prepared
IV, i

Since her rejection by her husband-to-be Angelo, Mariana has spent her time in solitary unhappiness, secluded in her estate with its surrounding moat.

The Duke, still disguised as a friar, has come to visit her. When he arrives, she is listening to a sad song sung by a young servant boy. The song tells of a disloyal lover:

> Take, o take those lips away
>   that so sweetly were forsworn,[1]
> And those eyes, the break of day,
>   lights that do mislead the morn;[2]
> But my kisses bring again,[3]
>   bring again;
> Seals[4] of love, but seal'd in vain,
>   seal'd in vain.

[1] *that lied to me so sweetly*
[2] *those eyes, as beautiful as the dawn, which trick the early morning into thinking that the sun has risen*
[3] *give back*
[4] *declarations, promises*

Mariana apologises, assuring the Duke that she was not listening to music light-heartedly. Rather than encouraging her to be cheerful, the song had the effect of soothing her sorrow:

> *Mariana:* I cry you mercy,[1] sir, and well could wish
> You had not found me here so musical.
> Let me excuse me, and believe me so;
> My mirth it much displeas'd, but pleas'd my woe.

[1] *I beg your pardon*

The Duke mentions that he is expecting to meet someone shortly, and at this moment Isabella arrives. The Duke asks Mariana to leave the two of them for a few minutes.

Isabella reports that she has met with Angelo, as planned, to agree to his proposition. They are to meet in his garden, in secret, in the dead of night. The garden is enclosed by a wall, and can only be reached from a vineyard which itself is protected by a wooden fence. Angelo has given her the two keys needed to open the gates, first to the vineyard and then to the hidden garden.

The Duke now calls Mariana back. He asks her to confirm that she trusts him, and then introduces her to Isabella, explaining that the visitor has a plan that will be of interest to her. The two women go aside to discuss the scheme, and when they return the Duke is gratified to hear that Mariana is keen to go ahead with it.

Isabella reminds Mariana that, after their lovemaking, she is to mention the promised pardon for Claudio; however, she must speak in a whisper so as not to give away her true identity. The Duke, finally, assures Mariana that, in taking Isabella's place, she will not be doing anything morally wrong:

Isabella: Little have you to say
When you depart from him, but, soft and low,
'Remember now my brother'.
Mariana: Fear me not.[1]
Duke: Nor, gentle daughter, fear you not at all.
He is your husband on a pre-contract:[2]
To bring you thus together 'tis no sin ...

[1] *don't worry; I won't let you down*
[2] *promise, commitment to marry in the future*

Pompey finds a new career   IV, ii

It is midnight. Pompey, now in prison for soliciting customers for Mistress Overdone's brothel, is approached by the provost. There is a problem in the prison, he explains; the executioner is busy, and needs an assistant. If Pompey agrees to take on the job, he will escape the punishment that has been planned for him:

> *Provost:* Here is in our prison a common executioner, who in his office[1] lacks a helper; if you will take it on you to assist him, it shall redeem you from your gyves:[2] if not, you shall have your full time of imprisonment, and your deliverance with an unpitied whipping[3] ...
>
> [1] *role, work*
> [2] *chains, shackles*
> [3] *you will be whipped mercilessly before your release*

Pompey accepts the offer immediately, and the provost calls in Abhorson, the executioner, to meet his helper. If his new colleague proves useful, says the provost, Abhorson can employ him permanently. Pompey may claim that he is too good for this line of work; if so, he should be ignored. The provost likewise dismisses Abhorson's anxiety about associating with a pimp:

> *Provost:* Sirrah, here's a fellow will help you tomorrow in your execution ... He cannot plead his estimation[1] with you: he hath been a bawd.
> *Abhorson:* A bawd, sir? Fie upon him, he will discredit our mystery.[2]
> *Provost:* Go to, sir, you weigh equally: a feather will turn the scale.[3]
>
> [1] *assert his superior status*
> [2] *bring the trade of executioner into disrepute*
> [3] *your reputations are as bad as each other*

The two men eventually agree to work together, and Abhorson takes his new apprentice away for further instruction.

Claudio's life in the balance

The provost calls for the two condemned men. One is a murderer named Barnardine, and the other is Claudio. When Claudio arrives, the provost shows him his death warrant; the sentence is to be carried out this coming morning. Barnardine, reports Claudio, is sleeping so soundly that he cannot be woken. With a final word of comfort, the provost sends Claudio back to his cell.

The hooded figure of the Duke now arrives at the prison. He hopes to hear that, following Mariana's assignation with Angelo, the promised pardon for Claudio has been issued. The provost tells him that there have been no messages or visitors all night; the Duke maintains that good news is on its way, and is relieved when a messenger from Angelo arrives at the prison. He is confident that his plan has worked:

> Duke: [*aside*] This is his pardon, purchas'd by such sin
> For which the pardoner himself is in.[1]
>
> [1] *obtained through the same crime for which Angelo is prosecuting Claudio*

The messenger hands a note to the provost, stating that Angelo has given strict instructions that the orders it contains must be followed to the letter. The contents of the note come as a terrible shock to the Duke:

> Provost: [*reads*] *Whatsoever you may hear to the contrary, let Claudio be executed by four of the clock* [1] ... *For my better satisfaction, let me have Claudio's head sent me by five ... fail not to do your office, as you will answer it at your peril.*[2]
>
> [1] *four o'clock in the morning*
> [2] *if you fail to carry out your task, your life will be in danger*

55

> "*Shakespeare's play shares some of its plot elements with his comedies – thwarted courtship, disguise, bawdy humour; while others – violence threatened and executed, the illicit use of power by subordinates – are derived from his tragic dramas.* Measure for Measure *stages the interweaving of sexuality, morality and power ... It is a play that is as timely and resonant in the early decades of the 21st century as it was at the beginning of the 17th or end of the 19th century.*"
>
> Kate Chedzgoy, Measure for Measure: *What's the Problem?*, 2016

Thinking quickly, the Duke asks about Barnardine, the murderer due to be executed later in the day. He has been a prisoner for many years, says the provost, but evidence has recently come to light that proves his guilt beyond doubt. The man seems completely unconcerned about his fate:

Duke: Hath he borne himself penitently in prison? How seems he to be touched?
Provost: A man that apprehends death no more dreadfully but [1] as a drunken sleep; careless, reckless, and fearless of what's past, present, or to come: insensible of mortality, and desperately mortal. [2]
Duke: He wants advice. [3]
Provost: He will hear none. He hath evermore had the liberty of the prison: [4] give him leave to escape hence, he would not.

[1] *than*
[2] *with no thought for his impending death, even though his sins have put his soul in danger*
[3] *he is in need of spiritual guidance*
[4] *he has always been free to wander around the prison*

The Duke now confides in the provost: he knows for certain that Claudio is no more guilty than Angelo himself. However, he needs time to prove this, and he asks the provost to delay Claudio's execution for four days.

The provost, fearing for his own life, insists that he cannot disobey Angelo's command; Claudio's head must be delivered to him in a matter of hours. The Duke suggests an alternative, giving his word, as a holy friar, that the provost will be safe:

Provost: ... I may make my case as Claudio's to cross this in the smallest.[1]

Duke: By the vow of mine order, I warrant you, if my instructions may be your guide: let this Barnardine be this morning executed, and his head borne to Angelo.

[1] *if I deviate from Angelo's command in the slightest, my fate will be the same as Claudio's*

The provost protests that Angelo will know that the substituted head is not Claudio's. The Duke disagrees: the head can be shaved and disfigured in various ways to make it difficult to identify precisely.

Realising that the provost is still reluctant, the Duke goes even further. He asks how he would react if he received word not from Angelo but from the Duke himself. The provost replies that the idea is too unlikely to be worth considering. At this point the Duke shows him a letter:

Duke: Look you, sir, here is the hand and seal[1] of the Duke: you know the character,[2] I doubt not, and the signet is not strange to you?

Provost: I know them both.

[1] *emblem made by pressing a signet ring into sealing wax*
[2] *handwriting*

The letter confirms that, unbeknown to Angelo, the Duke is to return to Vienna shortly. The provost, thrown into confusion by the letter and by the friar's apparent acquaintance with the Duke, agrees to go along with the plan: Claudio's head will be replaced by that of Barnardine.

Barnardine is unprepared   IV, iii

Surrounded by familiar faces, Pompey feels thoroughly at home in his new job at the prison. Many of the imprisoned debtors, petty criminals and quarrelsome young gallants are regulars at Mistress Overdone's brothel:

> *Pompey:* I am as well acquainted [1] here as I was in our house of profession: one would think it were Mistress Overdone's own house, for here be many of her old customers.
>
> [1] *I have as many friends*

The executioner Abhorson arrives: the time has come for Barnardine to die, as ordered by the provost. Abhorson and Pompey call out for the condemned man. He is angry at being disturbed so early in the morning:

> *Pompey:* You must rise and be hanged, Master Barnardine.
> *Abhorson:* What hoa, Barnardine!
> *Barnardine:* [*from his cell*] A pox o' your throats! Who makes that noise there? What are you?
> *Pompey:* Your friends, sir, the hangman. You must be so good, sir, to rise and be put to death.
> *Barnardine:* Away, you rogue, away; I am sleepy.

Barnardine eventually emerges from his cell. He greets Abhorson warmly; the two have known one another for many years. However, he is annoyed to hear that the warrant for his execution has come this morning. He has been drinking all night, he explains, and is no fit state to die.

The arrival of a friar, who has come to give Barnardine spiritual guidance, does nothing to change his mind. He refuses flatly to take part in the execution:

> *Barnardine:* ... I will not consent to die this day, that's certain.
> *Duke:* O sir, you must; and therefore I beseech you
> Look forward on the journey you shall go.
> *Barnardine:* I swear I will not die today for any man's persuasion.[1]
> *Duke:* But hear you –
> *Barnardine:* Not a word. If you have anything to say to me, come to my ward:[2] for thence will not I today.[3]
>
> [1] *no matter who tries to persuade me*
> [2] *cell*
> [3] *I'm not moving from it today*

With that, Barnardine marches resolutely back to his cell.

The provost now returns, expecting to find the execution of Barnardine in progress. The Duke reports that the prisoner is drunk, unrepentant, and completely unprepared for death. It would be a sin, he asserts, to execute him in his current state.

> *"The state must defer his dying until he has been persuaded to accept it willingly, otherwise the punishment will have no point. Unless Barnardine somehow 'performs' his own death, it will not constitute an event in his life and so will discredit the law that has inflicted it upon him. There is no more effective resistance to power than genuinely not caring about it, since power only lives in exacting a response of obedience from its victims."*
>
> Terry Eagleton, *William Shakespeare*, 1986

A timely death

The provost mentions that another prisoner, Ragozine, died of natural causes earlier this morning. By chance, this criminal resembles Claudio much more closely than does Barnardine.

The Duke is delighted; Ragozine's severed head will surely persuade Angelo that his instructions have been carried out. The head must be removed and sent immediately:

> *Provost:*   Here in the prison, father,
> There died this morning of a cruel fever
> One Ragozine, a most notorious pirate,
> A man of Claudio's years; his beard and head
> Just of his colour. What if we do omit
> This reprobate till he were well inclin'd,[1]
> And satisfy the deputy with the visage
> Of Ragozine, more like to Claudio?[2]
> *Duke:*   O, 'tis an accident that heaven provides.
> Dispatch it presently …
>
> [1] *forget about Barnardine until he is properly prepared for death*
> [2] *satisfy Angelo by sending him the head of Ragozine, who looks more like Claudio*

> *"Angelo demands proof that Claudio has been executed, and it is proposed instead that a drunken murderer, Barnardine, be executed in his stead. But Barnardine, unlike Mariana, will not go along with this substitutive plan: he does not want to be a bit-player in the Duke's moral melodrama. One effect of Barnardine's comically unrepentant resistance is to focus attention on the play's theme of substitution – because this substitute has himself to be substituted."*
>
> Emma Smith, Measure for Measure: *Symmetry and Substitution*, 2016

To make sure that news of their subterfuge does not escape to the outside world, the Duke tells the provost to lock away both Claudio and Barnardine in secret cells for the time being. He assures the provost that everything will be resolved safely within the next day or two, and sends him away to obtain the substitute head.

When the provost has left, the Duke reveals that he intends to write to his deputy to announce his imminent return to Vienna. He will ask Angelo to meet him, in public, outside the city. They will then walk back to Vienna, together, in formal procession.

At the same time, the Duke hints that Angelo will be subject to the full, impartial force of the law for his offences:

> Duke: ... By cold gradation and well-balanc'd form,[1]
> We shall proceed with[2] Angelo.
>
> [1] *calmly, step by step, and observing the proper procedures*
> [2] *walk with; also deal with, prosecute*

The provost returns briefly, carrying Ragozine's severed head. The Duke hurries him away to deliver it to Angelo as soon as possible.

Lucio is indiscreet

Isabella now arrives at the prison. She has come to see her brother, trusting that Angelo has pardoned him as promised. The Duke decides not to tell her yet of the scheme that has saved Claudio's life:

> *Duke:* ... I will keep her ignorant of her good,[1]
> To make her heavenly comforts of despair
> When it is least expected.
>
> [1] *unaware of her good fortune*

When she hears of Angelo's treachery, Isabella is devastated:

> *Isabella:* Hath yet the deputy sent my brother's pardon?
> *Duke:* He hath releas'd him, Isabel – from the world.
> His head is off, and sent to Angelo.
> *Isabella:* Nay, but it is not so!
> *Duke:* It is no other. Show your wisdom, daughter
> In your close patience.[1]
> *Isabella:* O, I will to him and pluck out his eyes!
> *Duke:* You shall not be admitted to his sight.
>
> [1] *by bearing your affliction with self-control*

The Duke does his best to comfort Isabella. A senior member of his own religious order, he assures her, has told him that the Duke of Vienna himself is about to return to the city. When this happens, Isabella will have the chance to tell the world about Angelo's true character.

The Duke instructs Isabella to visit Friar Peter at the monastery, with the message that the two friars are to meet this evening at Mariana's house. They will discuss Angelo's treatment of both Isabella and Mariana. Soon, on the Duke's return, Friar Peter will present Isabella to Angelo, in the presence of the Duke himself. There, she will be free to denounce Angelo, without reservation, to his superior.

As Isabella is leaving, Claudio's friend Lucio appears. Believing Claudio to have been executed, he offers his sympathy to Isabella. If the Duke had been in charge rather than his deputy, this would never have happened, he claims confidently; the Duke is an inveterate womaniser, and would have been more lenient. From under his disguise, the Duke responds tersely:

Lucio: ... By my troth, Isabel, I loved thy brother; if the old fantastical duke of dark corners[1] had been at home, he had lived.[2]

Duke: Sir, the Duke is marvellous little beholding to your reports;[3] but the best is, he lives not in them.[4]

Lucio: Friar, thou knowest not the Duke so well as I do. He's a better woodman[5] than thou tak'st him for.

[1] *the capricious old Duke, who is often involved in secret assignations*
[2] *Claudio would have lived*
[3] *doesn't take the slightest interest in your stories*
[4] *they do not depict him as he really is*
[5] *hunter of women*

> *... the old fantastical duke of dark corners ...*
>
> "*While the bulk of what Lucio says is nonsense, this phrase is the most accurate description of the Duke that the play affords.*"
>
> Northrop Frye, *On Shakespeare*, 1986

The Duke leaves, exasperated, but the talkative Lucio insists on accompanying him. He recounts how he once stood trial before the Duke, accused of getting one of Mistress Overdone's prostitutes pregnant. He denied the charge, of course, though in reality he was guilty. Admitting the truth would have meant a forced marriage:

> *Lucio:* I was once before him for getting a wench with child.
> *Duke:* Did you such a thing?
> *Lucio:* Yes, marry,[1] did I; but I was fain to forswear it;[2] they would else have married me to the rotten medlar.[3]
>
> [1] *indeed*
> [2] *I was obliged to deny it*
> [3] *decaying old fruit, whore*

Lucio is determined to keep his new friend company despite his objections; he has plenty more stories to tell about the Duke, he promises.

Angelo agonises   IV, iv

Angelo and Escalus have just received the latest of a series of letters from the Duke. They are puzzled; the various messages seem confused and contradictory, and suggest that the Duke may even be mentally unstable.

The Duke's latest letter, however, is clear. He is returning to Vienna, and wishes to meet Angelo and Escalus at the gates of the city, where his authority will be officially handed back. He also commands them to make a proclamation in advance of his return: any citizens with outstanding grievances must present their case, in public, to the returning Duke.

Angelo sends his second in command away to make the necessary preparations for the Duke's arrival. Alone, he contemplates his violation of Isabella with dismay:

> Angelo: This deed unshapes me quite;[1] makes me unpregnant
> And dull[2] to all proceedings. A deflower'd maid;
> And by an eminent body, that enforc'd
> The law against it![3]
>
> [1] *has left me utterly bewildered*
> [2] *unfit and inattentive*
> [3] *by an important official, one who enforced the law against fornication*

Fortunately, he reflects, Isabella will not accuse him in public. Her own shame at losing her virginity will prevent her; besides, she must realise that his upright reputation places him beyond the reach of scandal.

Claudio's execution, too, is on Angelo's mind. It was fear of retribution, he reveals, that led him to renege on his agreement with Isabella; if the young man had discovered that his sister had sacrificed her virginity in return for his life, he might have reacted violently. Nevertheless, Angelo is tormented by his decision:

> Angelo: He should have liv'd:
> Save that his riotous youth, with dangerous sense,[1]
> Might in the times to come have ta'en revenge
> By so receiving a dishonour'd life
> With ransom of such shame.[2] Would yet[3] he had lived.
>
> [1] *passion, spirit*
> [2] *for gaining his reprieve through such a shameful bargain*
> [3] *I still wish*

Angelo realises that his own actions have led him to a state of utter despair:

Angelo: Alack, when once our grace [1] we have forgot,
Nothing goes right; we would, and we would not.[2]

[1] *our better qualities; the principles of our faith*
[2] *we have conflicting desires and intentions; we lose our sense of right and wrong*

> "Here we enter one of Shakespeare's themes ... that an evil act will solve nothing. It will lead to more and greater evil acts ... Measure for Measure is arguably Shakespeare's most theological play."
>
> Nicholas Fogg, *Hidden Shakespeare*, 2013

Final preparations IV, v – vi

The Duke, preparing for his public return, has come to see Friar Peter. He gives the friar letters for various citizens of Vienna, containing instructions for the ceremony that will mark his arrival.

Isabella and Mariana, meanwhile, are already waiting near the city gates. Isabella is uneasy; the friar who has been counselling her has instructed her to accuse Angelo of forcing himself upon her, even though in reality Mariana took her place. She would prefer to tell the truth, that Angelo is a deceitful hypocrite, but decides that she should follow the friar's advice. Mariana agrees:

> *Isabella:* To speak so indirectly [1] I am loath;
> I would say the truth, but to accuse him so
> That is your part; [2] yet am I advis'd to do it,
> He says, to veil full purpose.[3]
> *Mariana:*   Be rul'd by him.

[1] *evasively, dishonestly*
[2] *your role will be to make the truth known*
[3] *to keep our strategy hidden*

The friar has also warned Isabella that he himself, if he appears before the Duke, may speak against her; but this is part of the plan, and she should not be deterred by any opposition.

Although he is unable to join the women himself, the friar has sent his fellow, Friar Peter, to bring them into the Duke's presence. Friar Peter now approaches, and informs them that the Duke is on his way. He knows of a place from which, despite the crowds, they will be able to attract the Duke's attention, and the three of them set off to the chosen location.

> *Measure for Measure* is a dark play. Much of the action takes place at night, or in confined, gloomy, obscure places; and secrecy and subterfuge pervade the plot. Finally, however, the drama emerges from the shadows:
>
> *"All of Acts II and III and much of Act IV take place within a prison or courthouse ... only the final scene of reconciliation takes place in a setting of openness and freedom – at the gates, the site of the Duke's ceremonious re-entry into Vienna."*
>
> Charles Boyce, *Shakespeare A to Z*, 1990

Isabella speaks out   V, i

At the gates of Vienna, the crowds are gathering for the return of the Duke. His deputy Angelo, Escalus, officials, lords, attendants and citizens are all assembled to greet their ruler, whose absence has been so mysterious.

The Duke, no longer in his friar's disguise, finally appears. Angelo and Escalus welcome him warmly, and in response he praises their virtuous governance of the city. He felt that he had to be reunited with them in the open, he explains, so that he could thank them publicly for their good work. His words to Angelo are not without irony:

> *Duke:* Many and hearty thankings to you both.
> We have made enquiry of you, and we hear
> Such goodness of your justice that our soul
> Cannot but yield you forth to public thanks,[1]
> Forerunning more requital.[2]
> *Angelo:* You make my bonds[3] still greater.
> *Duke:* O, but your desert speaks loud[4] ...
>
> [1] *I had no choice, in good conscience, but to thank you in public*
> [2] *in anticipation of greater rewards*
> [3] *my indebtedness to you*
> [4] *your deserving cries out to be acknowledged*

With Angelo on one side and Escalus on the other, the Duke walks towards the city. As he passes by, Friar Peter urges Isabella to make her appeal. The Duke, whose earlier proclamation expressly invited citizens to state their grievances, stops to listen:

> *Friar Peter:* Now is your time: speak loud, and kneel before him.
> *Isabella:* Justice, O royal Duke! Vail your regard [1]
> Upon a wrong'd – I would fain have said, a maid. [2]
> ... Justice! Justice! Justice!
> *Duke:* Relate your wrongs. In what? By whom? Be brief.
>
> [1] *look down, lower your gaze*
> [2] *a wronged virgin, I wish I could say*

The Duke calmly instructs her to direct her appeal to his deputy Angelo. She reacts with horror, and Angelo, realising what she is about to say, tries to forestall her accusations. She is not in her right mind, he explains, following Claudio's execution:

> *Isabella:* O worthy Duke,
> You bid me seek redemption of the devil. [1]
> Hear me yourself ...
> *Angelo:* My lord, her wits I fear me [2] are not firm.
> She hath been a suitor to me [3] for her brother,
> Cut off [4] by course of justice.
> *Isabella:* By course of justice!
> *Angelo:* And she will speak most bitterly and strange.
>
> [1] *it would be like asking the devil to save my soul*
> [2] *I'm afraid, unfortunately*
> [3] *she has asked for my help*
> [4] *executed*

She proceeds to launch a series of allegations at Angelo: he is a cheat, a murderer, an abuser and a hypocrite. The Duke asks sympathetically for her to be taken away: she is obviously deranged, as Angelo has suggested.

Determined to be heard, Isabella presses on, insisting that she is perfectly sane. It may seem improbable, she accepts, that Angelo is as wicked as her portrayal suggests, but it is not impossible. People should not be deceived by the trappings of virtue and respectability:

> *Duke:* Away with her. Poor soul,
> She speaks this in th'infirmity of sense.
> *Isabella:* ... Make not impossible
> That which but seems unlike.[1] 'Tis not impossible
> But one, the wicked'st caitiff on the ground,[2]
> May seem as shy, as grave, as just, as absolute[3]
> As Angelo; even so may Angelo,
> In all his dressings, caracts, titles, forms,[4]
> Be an arch-villain. Believe it, royal Prince ...
>
> [1] *something that merely seems unlikely*
> [2] *the most wicked villain on earth*
> [3] *strict*
> [4] *his formal garments and badges of authority, his status and rituals of high office*

For someone who is mad, the Duke remarks ironically, this woman seems perfectly capable of presenting a rational argument. He asks Isabella to state her case. She describes her brother's crime and subsequent death sentence, and her decision to visit Angelo to ask for a reprieve.

> "The normal mechanisms of justice in Vienna having failed her, Isabella here attempts to get round them and achieve a kind of moral justice that lies outside the scope of legal process by appealing directly to the ruler. The cry of her solitary female voice is dramatically juxtaposed with the staging of patriarchal civic spectacle."
>
> Kate Chedzgoy, Measure for Measure: What's the Problem?, 2016

To the Duke's irritation, Lucio is determined to get involved in the proceedings:

Isabella: I – in probation of a sisterhood[1] –
Was sent to by my brother; one Lucio
As then the messenger.
Lucio: That's I, and't like[2] your Grace.
I came to her from Claudio, and desir'd her
To try her gracious fortune with Lord Angelo
For her poor brother's pardon.
Isabella: That's he indeed.
Duke: [*to Lucio*] You were not bid to speak.
Lucio: No, my good lord,
Nor wish'd to hold my peace.
Duke: I wish you now, then;
Pray you take note of it …

[1] *a novice preparing to become a nun*
[2] *if it please*

Isabella continues with her account. However, as instructed by the friar, she does not mention that Mariana, unbeknown to Angelo, secretly took her place at their night-time assignation:

Isabella: … the vile conclusion
I now begin with grief and shame to utter.
He would not, but[1] by gift of my chaste body
To his concupiscible[2] intemperate lust,
Release my brother; and after much debatement,
My sisterly remorse confutes mine honour,[3]
And I did yield to him.

[1] *except, other than*
[2] *passionate, uncontrollable*
[3] *my concern for Claudio, as his sister, overcame my determination to remain chaste*

Even though she gave in to Angelo's demands, she asserts, he ordered the execution to go ahead.

71

The Duke claims that her story is far-fetched and malicious. Angelo is renowned for his integrity, he points out; besides, it would make no sense for Angelo to punish her brother for a crime that he himself had committed. She has clearly been influenced by someone with bad intentions.

At this point Isabella admits defeat. As she had feared, the Duke is clearly not going to believe her. She realises that she will be imprisoned for her slander, and as the Duke's guards take her away she resigns herself to her fate:

>   *Isabella:* ... Heaven shield your Grace from woe,
>   As I, thus wrong'd, hence unbelieved go.

A mysterious friar

The Duke declares that there has undoubtedly been a plot against Angelo: this is a serious matter, and must be investigated. As Isabella is escorted away, he demands to know the name of the conspirator who persuaded her to make these false accusations. She mentions the friar, named Lodowick, who did his best to save her brother.

Lucio confirms the man's identity. However, even though he was a friar, he was devious and untrustworthy, Lucio reveals. Indeed, he could hardly restrain himself from punching the man for insulting the Duke:

>   *Duke:* Who knew of your intent and coming hither?
>   *Isabella:* One that I would[1] were here, Friar Lodowick.
>   *Duke:* A ghostly father, belike.[2] Who knows that Lodowick?
>   *Lucio:* My lord, I know him. 'Tis a meddling friar;
>   I do not like the man; had he been lay,[3] my lord,
>   For certain words he spake against your Grace
>   In your retirement,[4] I had swing'd him[5] soundly.

>   [1] *wish*
>   [2] *a friar who no doubt operates secretly, under cover of darkness*
>   [3] *if he had not been a holy man*
>   [4] *absence*
>   [5] *I would have thrashed him*

This friar must be found urgently, announces the Duke: he has not only plotted against his deputy, but slandered the Duke himself. Lucio volunteers the information that he has seen friar Lodowick very recently. He hints that there may have been something improper going on between the friar and Isabella:

Duke: Let this friar be found.
Lucio: But yesternight,[1] my lord, she and that friar,
I saw them at the prison: a saucy[2] friar,
A very scurvy[3] fellow.

[1] *only last night*
[2] *impudent, lecherous*
[3] *repugnant, detestable*

At this point Friar Peter intervenes. He knows Friar Lodowick, he declares, and Lucio's description bears no resemblance to the man himself, who is honest, principled and devout. Unfortunately Friar Lodowick cannot be present to defend himself:

Friar Peter: I know him for[1] a man divine and holy ...
... a man that never yet
Did, as he vouches,[2] misreport your Grace.
Lucio: My lord, most villainously; believe it.
Friar Peter: Well, he in time may come to clear himself;
But at this instant he is sick, my lord:
Of a strange fever.

[1] *I know him to be*
[2] *as Lucio states*

Friar Peter now reveals that he has been sent by the absent Friar Lodowick to speak in Angelo's defence. Isabella has not been telling the truth, he announces. Angelo did not have intercourse with her, and he can prove it.

The Duke turns to Angelo; this is good news for him, he remarks. He criticises the culprits for their arrogance, but his words are ambiguous:

> *Friar Peter:* ... To justify this worthy nobleman[1]
> So vulgarly and personally accus'd,
> Her[2] shall you hear disproved to her eyes,
> Till she herself confess it.
> *Duke:* Good friar, let's hear it.
> Do you not smile at this, Lord Angelo?
> O heaven, the vanity of wretched fools!
>
> [1] *prove Angelo innocent*
> [2] *Isabella*

Friar Peter calls for his witness, and a veiled figure appears.

"Shakespeare sets the entire play in an atmosphere of sin ... The Vienna of the background seems to be a city of brothels and bawds; the outlaw characters revel in sexuality, yet not freely – their speeches contain a note of prurience and lip-licking lasciviousness ... The other characters suffer to varying degrees from a sense of the sinfulness of sex ... Indeed, it is not just authority which is tried in Measure for Measure: *it is sexuality itself that is on trial."*

Marilyn French, *Shakespeare's Division of Experience*, 1981

A promise is recalled

The woman beneath the veil is Mariana. The Duke asks her to show her face, but she refuses. Her answers are enigmatic:

> *Mariana:* Pardon, my lord; I will not show my face
> Until my husband bid me.
> *Duke:* What, are you married?
> *Mariana:* No, my lord.
> *Duke:* Are you a maid?
> *Mariana:* No, my lord.
> *Duke:* A widow, then?
> *Mariana:* Neither, my lord.

She continues in the same vein, with bawdy interruptions from Lucio:

> *Mariana:* My lord, I do confess I ne'er was married;
> And I confess besides, I am no maid.
> I have known[1] my husband; yet my husband
> Knows not[2] that he ever knew me.
> *Lucio:* He was drunk then, my lord; it can be no better.[3]
> *Duke:* For the benefit of silence, would thou wert so too.[4]

> [1] *been intimate with*
> [2] *does not realise*
> [3] *there can be no better explanation*
> [4] *I wish you were drunk too, if it would keep you quiet*

The Duke asks what these riddles have to do with Angelo and the allegations against him. In accusing Angelo of fornication, says Mariana, Isabella is also accusing her husband. She knows that this is false; at the time when the crime is said to have taken place, Mariana's husband was in her arms, not with Isabella.

Angelo seizes on her words: perhaps Isabella is making the same false allegation against several men? Mariana contradicts him; only one man is involved, and that is Angelo himself.

75

Growing impatient, Angelo demands to see the woman's face. This time, Mariana does not refuse. She addresses Angelo directly:

> Mariana: [*removing her veil*] My husband bids me; now I will
> unmask.
> This is that face, thou cruel Angelo,
> Which once thou swor'st was worth the looking on:
> This is the hand which, with a vow'd contract,
> Was fast belock'd [1] in thine: this is the body
> That took away the match from Isabel [2]
> And did supply [3] thee at thy garden-house,
> In her imagin'd person. [4]
>
> [1] *clasped, as a token of our engagement*
> [2] *took Isabella's place in the planned assignation*
> [3] *satisfy*
> [4] *with the body that you imagined to be hers*

Angelo replies smoothly. He does not deny knowing the woman, but any suggestion of marriage was abandoned long ago. There was a problem with the amount of the dowry that had been promised; more seriously, he claims, he heard rumours that her moral standards might not be as high as he had believed:

> Angelo: My lord, I must confess I know this woman;
> And five years since, there was some speech of marriage
> Betwixt myself and her; which was broke off,
> Partly for that her promised proportions
> Came short of composition; [1] but in chief
> For that her reputation was disvalu'd
> In levity [2] ...
>
> [1] *because the financial assets that had originally been agreed were not available in full*
> [2] *because her reputation was cheapened due to her immoral behaviour*

Since that time, vows Angelo, he has had no contact whatsoever with Mariana. Once again, however, Mariana repeats her sworn declaration. Angelo is her pledged husband, and their contract has been sealed by their physical union:

> *Mariana:* ... I am affianc'd[1] this man's wife, as strongly
> As words could make up vows. And, my good lord,
> But Tuesday night last gone, in's garden house,
> He knew me as a wife.
>
> [1] *promised, engaged*

Angelo now becomes impatient. Some kind of conspiracy is clearly under way, and he demands the right to investigate it. The Duke gladly grants his wish:

> *Angelo:* ... good my lord, give me the scope of justice.
> My patience here is touch'd:[1] I do perceive
> These poor informal[2] women are no more
> But instruments of some more mightier member
> That sets them on.[3] Let me have my way, my lord,
> To find this practice[4] out.
> *Duke:* Ay, with my heart;
> And punish them to your height of pleasure.
>
> [1] *injured, hurt*
> [2] *unstable, deluded*
> [3] *are being used by some more powerful person who is influencing them*
> [4] *plot, scheme*

The Duke scolds Friar Peter and Mariana: along with Isabella, they are foolishly trying to damage the reputation of a worthy and respected lord. He instructs Escalus and Angelo to work together to look into the conspiracy. The chief suspect, however, is still missing:

> *Duke:* ... There is another friar that set them on;
> Let him be sent for.
> *Friar Peter:* Would he were here, my lord; for he indeed
> Hath set the women on to this complaint.

An attendant is sent off to find the shadowy Friar Lodowick. At this point the Duke excuses himself from the proceedings. With a final word of encouragement to Angelo to inflict suitable punishments on those who are plotting against him, he leaves.

The suspect is questioned

Escalus begins the investigation by questioning Lucio, who confirms that, despite outward appearances, the missing friar is deceitful and slanderous. Lucio will have his chance, promises Escalus, to denounce this elusive friar in person:

Escalus: Signior Lucio, did not you say you knew that Friar Lodowick to be a dishonest person?
Lucio: Cucullus non facit monachum:[1] honest in nothing but in his clothes, and one that hath spoke most villainous speeches of the Duke.
Escalus: We shall entreat you to abide here till he come, and enforce them against him.[2] We shall find this friar a notable fellow.

[1] *a proverb: 'a hood does not make a monk'*
[2] *accuse him of these crimes to his face*

Escalus then calls for Isabella to be brought back. When he asks for Angelo's permission to question her, Lucio cannot resist commenting suggestively on their alleged assignation:

Escalus: Call that same Isabel here once again ...
Pray you, my lord, give me leave to question; you shall see how I'll handle her.
Lucio: Not better than he, by her own report.

The provost arrives with Isabella, still surrounded by guards. With them is the Duke: but now he is disguised, once again, in a friar's habit.

It is difficult to establish precise dates for many of Shakespeare's plays, but *Measure for Measure* is widely regarded as the last comedy that he wrote. In the following years he was to produce tragic masterpieces such as *King Lear* and *Macbeth*, and later the more mystical romances such as *The Tempest*.

Why did Shakespeare stop writing comedies? Did he lose interest in the form? Was he responding to changing fashions? It has been pointed out that Richard Burbage – the leading actor in the King's Men, Shakespeare's theatre company – had become immensely popular by this time; he was the company's star performer, just as Shakespeare was their star writer. Burbage was perfectly suited to the weighty, powerful roles offered by tragedy, particularly as he got older, so the move away from comedy may have made sense both artistically and commercially.

Some scholars see more personal reasons behind the change, believing that the cynical, brooding atmosphere of *Measure for Measure* reveals a mood of disillusionment in which comedy was losing its appeal. Was Shakespeare, now aged forty, undergoing some sort of personal crisis – a long bout of depression, for example, or failing physical health?

"A considerable despair richly informs the play, and it is not unreasonable to suppose that the despair was Shakespeare's, at least imaginatively. I myself, rereading the play, hear in it an experiential exhaustion, a sense that desire has failed."

Harold Bloom, *Shakespeare: The Invention of the Human*, 1998

Escalus first addresses Isabella. He puts it to her that her claim to have visited Angelo in his garden is contradicted by Mariana's account. Before she can answer, however, attention is quickly diverted to the hooded figure who has arrived with her.

Lucio exclaims that this is the villainous Friar Lodowick who has caused so much trouble. When questioned, the man makes it clear that he is not overawed by the presence of the Duke's deputies:

> *Escalus:* Know you where you are?
> *Duke:* Respect to your great place;[1] and let the devil
> Be sometime honour'd for his burning throne.[2]
> Where is the Duke? 'Tis he should hear me speak.
> *Escalus:* The Duke's in us; and we will hear you speak ...
>
> [1] *office, position of authority*
> [2] *even the devil should be shown some respect for his status*

Turning to Isabella and Mariana, he offers his sympathy, remarking that they have no hope of obtaining justice in these circumstances. He goes on to criticise the Duke for being absent at this crucial moment. Lucio is delighted to have his allegations justified, while Escalus is appalled at the friar's insolence:

> *Duke:* ... O, poor souls,
> Come you to seek the lamb here of the fox?[1]
> Good-night to your redress![2] Is the Duke gone?
> Then is your cause gone too. The Duke's unjust
> Thus to retort your manifest appeal[3] ...
> *Lucio:* This is the rascal: this is he I spoke of.
> *Escalus:* Why, thou unreverend and unhallow'd[4] friar!
>
> [1] *to ask the fox to return your lost lamb*
> [2] *farewell to any chance of justice*
> [3] *to reject, by his absence, your case which is clearly valid*
> [4] *disrespectful and unholy*

Escalus quickly loses his temper. The friar has dragged two women into a plot to discredit the Duke's deputy, and has insulted the deputy to his face: now, to cap it all, he has stated that the Duke himself is uninterested in justice. He is clearly a dangerous individual, and the motive behind his actions must be extracted from him, with violence if necessary:

> *Escalus:* Take him hence! To th'rack[1] with him! – We'll touse you Joint by joint,[2] but we will know his purpose.
>
> [1] *instrument of torture*
> [2] *tear apart every joint in your body*

Friar Lodowick defends himself

The Duke announces that he cannot be tortured, as he is not a citizen, but a visitor to Vienna. During his time here, he has observed a great deal of wrongdoing:

> *Duke:* My business in this state
> Made me a looker-on here in Vienna,
> Where I have seen corruption boil and bubble
> Till it o'errun the stew[1] ...
>
> [1] *overflows from the pot; also, spills out from the brothels*

Escalus, still furious, accuses the friar of slandering the state, and demands that he be taken to prison. Angelo, however, decides to obtain more evidence against him. He asks Lucio what Friar Lodowick has said in private. Lucio enthusiastically steps forward to play the role of barrister:

> *Angelo:* What can you vouch against him, Signior Lucio?
> Is this the man that you did tell us of?
> *Lucio:* 'Tis he, my lord. – Come hither, goodman Baldpate,[1] do you know me?
>
> [1] *master Baldy (under his hood, the crown of a friar's head would normally be shaved)*

81

Lucio goes on to ask the friar's opinion of the Duke, claiming that the friar had insulted him outrageously. The Duke recalls that the opposite was the case. It was Lucio who had been free with his insults, calling the Duke a drunken womaniser among other things:

> *Lucio:* ... do you remember what you said of the Duke?
> *Duke:* Most notedly,[1] sir.
> *Lucio:* Do you so, sir? And was the Duke a fleshmonger,[2] a fool, and a coward, as you then reported him to be?
> *Duke:* You must, sir, change persons with me, ere you make that my report. You indeed spoke so of him, and much more, much worse ... I protest,[3] I love the Duke as I love myself.
>
> [1] *accurately, precisely*
> [2] *philanderer*
> [3] *declare*

Angelo observes that the friar, who had earlier criticised the Duke, seems to be changing his story. Escalus, impatient with the questioning, repeats his demand for the friar to be dragged away to prison, along with Isabella, Mariana and Friar Peter for good measure:

> *Angelo:* Hark how the villain would close[1] now, after his treasonable abuses!
> *Escalus:* Such a fellow is not to be talked withal.[2] Away with him to prison! Where is the provost? Away with him to prison! Lay bolts[3] enough upon him: let him speak no more. Away with those giglets[4] too, and with the other confederate companion![5]
>
> [1] *come to an agreement, placate us*
> [2] *with*
> [3] *shackles*
> [4] *those shameless women; Isabella and Mariana*
> [5] *their co-conspirator, Friar Peter*

The provost attempts to seize the Duke. With Angelo's encouragement, Lucio assists him, hurling insults at the prisoner as he does so:

> *Lucio:* Come, sir! ... Why, you bald-pated, lying rascal! – You must be hooded, must you? Show your knave's visage,[1] with a pox to you!

[1] *face*

Lucio angrily pulls off Friar Lodowick's hood. An amazed silence falls instantly over the assembled crowd as the Duke's face appears.

Angelo's downfall

The Duke turns first to the provost, asking him to release the three remaining prisoners. He then addresses Lucio, who is trying desperately to slip away unseen:

> *Duke:* Sneak not away, sir, for the friar and you
> Must have a word anon. – Lay hold on him.
> *Lucio:* [*aside*] This may prove worse than hanging.

Pardoning Escalus for his earlier outbursts, the Duke asks him to sit, and takes Angelo's place next to him. He then calmly asks Angelo, now standing before him, whether he has anything to say in his defence.

Angelo realises that he can no longer cover up his crimes; in his disguise as Friar Lodowick, the Duke has indisputable evidence both of his plan to rape Isabella and of his decision to have Claudio executed.

Resigned to his inevitable punishment, Angelo does not even wish to be tried in court. For the present, however, the Duke is concerned with Angelo's marriage, which he asks Friar Peter to perform without delay:

Angelo: ... good prince,
No longer session hold upon my shame,
But let my trial be mine own confession.[1]
Immediate sentence, then, and sequent death [2]
Is all the grace I beg.[3]
Duke: Come hither, Mariana.
– Say: wast thou e'er contracted to this woman?
Angelo: I was, my lord.
Duke: Go, take her hence, and marry her instantly.
Do you the office,[4] friar ...

[1] *do not hold legal proceedings over my shameful behaviour; let my full confession be my trial*
[2] *the death that will immediately follow*
[3] *the only mercy that I request*
[4] *perform the ceremony*

"Measure for Measure *is a play that seems to come of age in the 21st-century globalised world ... In every modern society it's possible to find examples of the social behaviour depicted in the play: rulers sometimes execute citizens for illegal sexual relationships; powerful men have been known to expect sexual favours in return for doing their jobs; and marriage is sometimes still imposed as a way of solving a social rather than a personal problem.*"

Kate McLuskie, *Gender in* Measure for Measure, 2016

The Duke now turns his attention to Isabella. He still has her interests at heart, he assures her, even though he is no longer disguised as a friar. She apologises for the trouble that, unaware of his status, she has caused him.

The Duke in turn apologises; had he revealed his true identity earlier, and exercised his authority, he might have saved her brother's life. Angelo's sudden decision to execute Claudio took him by surprise, and confounded his plan. He advises Isabella to accept Claudio's death philosophically, as he is now free from the cares of the world, and she agrees:

> *Duke:* But peace be with him.
> That life is better life, past fearing death,
> Than that which lives to fear.[1] Make it your comfort,
> So happy is your brother.[2]
> *Isabella:* I do, my lord.
>
> [1] *the life to come, where there is no more fear of death, is better than our life on earth, where fear of death is ever-present*
> [2] *that your brother is happy in this way*

At this point Angelo and Mariana, now married, return.

An eye for an eye

The Duke asks Isabella to forgive Angelo's intended violation of her, for the sake of his new wife. The killing of Claudio, however, is a different question. No matter how mercifully the law is applied, only one penalty is appropriate:

Duke: ... for your brother's life,
The very mercy of the law cries out
Most audible, even from his proper tongue: [1]
'An Angelo for Claudio; death for death.
Haste still pays haste,[2] and leisure answers leisure;
Like doth quit like,[3] and measure still for measure.'

[1] *even at its most merciful, the law itself cries out*
[2] *hasty actions are always met with hasty responses*
[3] *deeds must be repaid in kind*

... and measure still for measure.

The play's title might be taken simply to justify a suitable level of retaliation for all offences. The biblical text from which it is derived, however, has a very different tenor, suggesting that we should think carefully before taking action. The text, which would have been thoroughly familiar to Shakespeare and his audience, is from Jesus' Sermon on the Mount:

"Judge not, that ye be not judged. For with what judgement ye judge, ye shall be judged, and with what measure ye mete, it shall be measured unto you again. And why seest thou the mote that is in thy brother's eye, and perceivest not the beam that is in thine own eye?"

Gospel according to Matthew 7.1–3, Geneva Bible, 1576

Angelo's punishment, then, must fit the crime. Mariana is devastated:

Duke: We do condemn thee to the very block[1]
Where Claudio stoop'd to death, and with like[2] haste.
Away with him.
Mariana: O my most gracious lord,
I hope you will not mock me with a husband.[3]

[1] *executioner's block*
[2] *the same*
[3] *show contempt for me by giving me a husband in name only*

The Duke is adamant. Mariana's marriage to Angelo was necessary to preserve her reputation, he maintains, but the execution must still go ahead. The fact that Mariana will receive all his property is no consolation to her:

Duke: For his possessions,
Although by confiscation they are ours,[1]
We do instate and widow you with all,[2]
To buy you a better husband.
Mariana: O my dear lord,
I crave no other, nor no better man.

[1] *by law they should go to the state*
[2] *I endow you, as his widow, with all his property*

Mariana kneels in front of the Duke and implores him to let her husband live. To the Duke's amazement, she asks Isabella to do the same. She cannot, surely, expect Isabella to plead for the life of her brother's executioner:

Duke: Against all sense you do importune her.[1]
Should she kneel down in mercy of this fact,
Her brother's ghost his paved bed would break,[2]
And take her hence in horror.

[1] *your appeal goes against all reason and emotion*
[2] *would break out of his stone-covered tomb*

Mariana repeats her plea to Isabella. She is confident that Angelo will learn to become a better man in the future:

> *Mariana:* ... They say best men are moulded out of faults,
> And, for the most, become much more the better
> For being a little bad. So may my husband.
> O Isabel! Will you not lend a knee?

Isabella eventually agrees, and she adds her voice to Mariana's. Before he became obsessed with her, Isabella concludes, Angelo was motivated by his dedication to the law. And her brother, after all, did commit the crime for which he died:

> *Isabella:* [*kneeling*] Most bounteous sir:
> Look, if it please you, on this man condemn'd
> As if my brother liv'd. I partly think
> A due sincerity[1] govern'd his deeds
> Till he did look on me. Since it is so,
> Let him not die. My brother had but [2] justice,
> In that he did the thing for which he died ...

[1] *a fitting sense of devotion to duty*
[2] *only, nothing other than*

Even Angelo's plan to assault her can be set aside, she proposes, as an intention that did not eventually take place.

The Duke, unmoved, asks the two women to stand up; he will not hear any further appeals for leniency. Turning to the provost, he raises a different subject: why, he asks, was Claudio executed at such an early hour in the morning? The provost replies that this was done following a personal order from Angelo.

> ... Let him not die.
>
> "In the end, Mariana's virtue calls forth Isabella's, so that, despite the Duke's reminder of the code of family honour, Isabella joins in the appeal for her enemy's life. The chain-reaction whereby in the first part of the play three characters drew each other down into psychic disintegration is completely reversed, so that Mariana, Isabella, and Angelo achieve a mutual rehabilitation."
>
> J. W. Lever, Introduction to the Arden edition of *Measure for Measure*, 1965

The Duke is displeased when it emerges that the provost acted without official authorisation:

Duke: Provost, how came it Claudio was beheaded
At an unusual hour?
Provost: It was commanded so.
Duke: Had you a special warrant for the deed?
Provost: No, my good lord: it was by private message.
Duke: For which I do discharge you of your office.[1]
Give up your keys.

[1] *remove you from your position, dismiss you*

The provost asks for forgiveness; he was unsure at the time whether he should obey the command or not. In fact on reflection, he claims, he later decided not to execute the other prisoner mentioned in Angelo's note. This is borne out by the fact that the prisoner, Barnardine, is still alive.

The Duke calls for Barnardine to be brought before him: if only Claudio had been saved in the same way, he remarks sadly.

Mercy

As the provost leaves to summon Barnardine, Escalus tactfully expresses his sadness at his colleague's predicament. Angelo acknowledges that his actions have been unforgivable. He is overcome with regret, and neither expects nor wishes to be treated mercifully:

> *Escalus:* I am sorry one so learned and so wise
> As you, Lord Angelo, have still [1] appear'd,
> Should slip so grossly,[2] both in the heat of blood
> And lack of temper'd judgement afterward.
> *Angelo:* I am sorry that such sorrow I procure,[3]
> And so deep sticks it in my penitent heart
> That I crave death more willingly than mercy;
> 'Tis my deserving, and I do entreat it.[4]
>
> [1] *always*
> [2] *fall from grace so utterly*
> [3] *to cause such sorrow in other people*
> [4] *death is my deserved punishment, and I pray for it*

The provost returns, accompanying three individuals: the criminal Barnardine, the pregnant Juliet, who had been engaged to Claudio, and a nameless blindfolded man.

The Duke has decided to pardon Barnardine, who is notoriously reckless, and has no thought for the safety of his soul. The Duke hopes that this act of mercy will make him consider his future more deeply, and asks Friar Peter to counsel him:

> *Duke:* … for those earthly faults, I quit [1] them all,
> And pray thee take this mercy to provide [2]
> For better times to come. Friar, advise him …
>
> [1] *forgive*
> [2] *prepare*

The moment that the Duke has long prepared for has now arrived. He asks the provost – who is playing his part in the Duke's scheme – to reveal the face of the mysterious prisoner. The provost removes the man's blindfold, remarking light-heartedly that he is the living image of Claudio.

The realisation that her brother is still alive is immediately followed by another surprise for the speechless Isabella as, without further ado, the Duke proposes to her:

> *Duke:* What muffl'd[1] fellow's that?
> *Provost:* This is another prisoner that I sav'd,
> Who should have died when Claudio lost his head;
> As like almost to Claudio as himself.[2] [*uncovers Claudio's face*]
> *Duke:* [*to Isabella*] If he be like your brother, for his sake
> Is he pardon'd; and for your lovely sake
> Give me your hand and say you will be mine.
> He is my brother too …
>
> [1] *covered, blindfolded*
> [2] *resembling Claudio almost as much as Claudio himself does*

Now that Claudio is revealed to be alive, even Angelo is affected by the air of joy, optimism and relief that has suffused the scene so unexpectedly. He senses that the Duke is in a forgiving mood, and he is quickly proved right:

> *Duke:* By this Lord Angelo perceives he's safe;
> Methinks I see a quickening[1] in his eye.
> Well, Angelo, your evil quits you well.[2]
> Look that you love your wife: her worth, worth yours.[3]
>
> [1] *reawakening, return to life*
> [2] *despite your wrongdoing, you have been well rewarded*
> [3] *strive to make your worth equal to hers*

There is another character, standing nearby, who requires the Duke's attention, one who has slandered him relentlessly. When asked to explain himself, Lucio can only offer a feeble excuse and beg not to be punished too harshly. The Duke brushes aside his request:

> *Duke:* ... yet here's one in place I cannot pardon.
> You, sirrah, that knew me for a fool, a coward,
> One all of luxury,[1] an ass, a madman:
> Wherein have I so deserv'd of you
> That you extol me thus?
> *Lucio:* Faith, my lord, I spoke it but according to the trick:[2] if you will hang me for it, you may: but I had rather it would please you I might be whipped.
> *Duke:* Whipp'd first, sir, and hang'd after.
>
> [1] *a man whose life was devoted to debauchery*
> [2] *custom, fashion*

"*After the pardon of two murderers, Lucio might be treated by the good Duke with less harshness; but perhaps the poet intended to show, what is too often seen, that men easily forgive wrongs which are not committed against themselves ...*"

Samuel Johnson, *The Plays of William Shakespeare*, 1765

The Duke now recalls that Lucio once boasted of getting one of Mistress Overdone's prostitutes pregnant. He confided in his companion, the friar, that he had lied to the Duke about his offence, and had escaped without punishment. He will not escape this time, declares the Duke. For whatever remains of Lucio's life, Kate Keepdown is to become his wife:

> *Duke:* Proclaim it, provost, round about the city,
> If any woman wrong'd by this lewd fellow,
> – As I have heard him swear himself there's one
> Whom he begot with child – let her appear,
> And he shall marry her. The nuptial finish'd,
> Let him be whipp'd and hang'd.

Lucio implores the Duke to change his mind. He replies that he is prepared to call off the whipping and hanging, but the marriage must go ahead. If Lucio considers it a punishment, it is a just one:

> *Duke:* Upon mine honour, thou shalt marry her.
> Thy slanders I forgive, and therewithal
> Remit thy other forfeits [1] ...
> *Lucio:* Marrying a punk,[2] my lord, is pressing to death,[3]
> Whipping, and hanging.
> *Duke:*   Slandering a prince deserves it.

[1] *I will cancel your other penalties accordingly*
[2] *prostitute*
[3] *execution by crushing under heavy weights*

Lucio is dragged away to prison to await his enforced marriage, and his future life with Kate Keepdown.

One of the many puzzling aspects of *Measure for Measure* is its abrupt, enigmatic ending. Once Lucio's punishment has been announced, the play's final words all belong to the Duke; the other characters' responses are all wordless. For example, how does Isabella react to seeing Claudio alive? And how does she answer the Duke's proposal? These are decisions for the director and actors; the text provides no clues. Some critics see a profound significance in Isabella's silence:

"Isabella is confronted with a series of overwhelming events: a living Claudio appears, the Duke proposes marriage, and Angelo is pardoned. All of Isabella's main assumptions – that Angelo was condemned, that the Duke was a committed celibate, that her brother was dead, and that she herself would remain chaste for life – are challenged, if not negated, in the space of five lines. She remains speechless, a baffled actress who has run out of lines. The gradual loss of her personal voice during the course of the play has become, finally, a literal loss of voice. In this sense, Measure for Measure *is Isabella's tragedy."*

Marcia Riefer, *The Constriction of Female Power in* Measure for Measure, 1984

New beginnings

It is time to return to Vienna and its daily life, under the rule once again of Duke Vincentio. His brief but eventful experience concealed under the friar's hood has given him a new, richer perspective on those around him; and before the assembled company make their way back through the city gates, the Duke has some final words of encouragement for his companions.

He turns first to Claudio and Juliet:

Duke: She, Claudio, that you wrong'd, look you restore.[1]

[1] be sure to compensate her; marry her

He then wishes Mariana and Angelo every happiness:

Duke: Joy to you, Mariana; love her, Angelo:
I have confess'd her,[1] and I know her virtue.

[1] *spoken to her heart to heart, in my disguise as a friar*

Escalus has shown himself to be completely trustworthy, and will be rewarded for his service:

Duke: Thanks, good friend Escalus, for thy much goodness;
There's more behind that is more gratulate.[1]

[1] *there are greater rewards to come that will express my gratitude*

The provost, too, has been thoughtful and diligent, and will no longer be confined to his role in the prison:

Duke: Thanks, provost, for thy care and secrecy;
We shall employ thee in a worthier place.[1]

[1] *give you a better, more appropriate position*

Finally, the Duke repeats his request to his new-found love:

Duke: Dear Isabel,
I have a motion much imports your good;[1]
Whereto if you'll a willing ear incline,[2]
What's mine is yours, and what is yours is mine.

[1] *a proposal that is greatly to your benefit*
[2] *if you will consider my suggestion favourably*

The Duke announces that he wishes to return to his palace: there is much to talk about, and much still to reveal. He leads the gathered citizens back through the gates, towards the city.

Acknowledgements

The following publications have proved invaluable as sources of factual information and critical insight:

- Anne Barton, Programme notes for *Measure for Measure*, RSC Publications, 1970

- Jonathan Bate, *Soul of the Age*, Penguin, 2009

- Harold Bloom, *Shakespeare: The Invention of the Human*, Riverhead Books, 1998

- Charles Boyce, *Shakespeare A to Z*, Roundtable Press, 1990

- Kate Chedzgoy, Measure for Measure: *What's the Problem?*, from *Discovering Literature*, British Library, 2016

- Andrew Dickson, *Royal Shakespeare: A Playwright and his King*, from *Discovering Literature*, British Library, 2016

- Terry Eagleton, *William Shakespeare*, Blackwell, 1986

- Nicholas Fogg, *Hidden Shakespeare*, Amberley Publishing, 2013

- Marilyn French, *Shakespeare's Division of Experience*, Simon & Schuster, 1981

- Northrop Frye, *On Shakespeare*, Yale University Press, 1986

- Harold C. Goddard, *The Meaning of Shakespeare*, University of Chicago Press, 1951

- J. W. Lever, Introduction to the Arden edition of *Measure for Measure*, Methuen, 1965

- Laurie Maguire and Emma Smith, *30 Great Myths About Shakespeare*, Wiley-Blackwell, 2013

- Kate McLuskie, *Gender in* Measure for Measure, from *Discovering Literature*, British Library, 2016

- John Mullan, Measure for Measure *and Punishment*, from *Discovering Literature*, British Library, 2016

- Marcia Riefer, *The Constriction of Female Power in* Measure for Measure, from *Shakespeare Quarterly*, Oxford University Press, 1984

- Emma Smith, Measure for Measure: *Symmetry and Substitution*, from *Discovering Literature*, British Library, 2016

- Gary Taylor, *Reinventing Shakespeare*, Hogarth Press, 1990

All quotations from *Measure for Measure* are taken from the Arden Shakespeare.

Guides currently available in the *Shakespeare Handbooks* series are:

- **Antony & Cleopatra** (ISBN 978 1 899747 02 3, £4.95)
- **As You Like It** (ISBN 978 1 899747 00 9, £4.95)
- **Hamlet** (ISBN 978 1 899747 07 8, £4.95)
- **Henry IV, Part 1** (ISBN 978 1 899747 05 4, £4.95)
- **Julius Caesar** (ISBN 978 1 899747 11 5, £4.95)
- **King Lear** (ISBN 978 1 899747 03 0, £4.95)
- **Macbeth** (ISBN 978 1 899747 04 7, £4.95)
- **Measure for Measure** (ISBN 978 1 899747 14 6, £4.95)
- **The Merchant of Venice** (ISBN 978 1 899747 13 9, £4.95)
- **A Midsummer Night's Dream** (ISBN 978 1 899747 09 2, £4.95)
- **Othello** (ISBN 978 1 899747 12 2, £4.95)
- **Romeo & Juliet** (ISBN 978 1 899747 10 8, £4.95)
- **The Tempest** (ISBN 978 1 899747 08 5, £4.95)
- **Twelfth Night** (ISBN 978 1 899747 01 6, £4.95)

www.shakespeare-handbooks.com

Details correct at time of going to press. Whilst every effort is made to keep prices low, Upstart Crow Publications reserves the right to show new retail prices on covers which may differ from those previously advertised in the text or elsewhere.